Lamentations of a Dad

How Takeaways Led to Comebacks

Gene Nalbandian

Halo ●●●●
Publishing International

ISBN: 978-1-61244-453-6
Library of Congress Control Number: 2016903220

Printed in the United States of America

Published by Halo Publishing International
1100 NW Loop 410
Suite 700 - 176
San Antonio, Texas 78213
Toll Free 1-877-705-9647
Website: www.halopublishing.com
E-mail: contact@halopublishing.com

I dedicate this book to my children—Stephan, Jon David, Michelle, and Jeanne—and to families afflicted by drug addiction.

Contents

Foreword

Gene Nalbandian is a friend of mine. In reading his *Lamentations of a Dad,* I realized I was reading a story of the human condition and of the suffering of the human family. Gene's heritage is within the Armenian-American family. He grew up with the memory of the suffering of his people in the Armenian genocide in the early part of the twentieth century. His family, having suffered with a history of persecution, came to America for a new beginning in hard work, religious freedom, economic opportunity, and escape from their confrontation with evil in the old world.

Gene's life is one of native charisma, intellectual giftedness, athletic achievement, and economic accomplishment. He shares his successes and failures, his joys and sorrows, and his own efforts to find the meaning of it all. It is a story of what Frederick Buechner named a journey in search of a person to be, others to love, and work to do. But beyond that it is a story of a search for God to give meaning and purpose to life, even to the angst and evil of the human heart.

Lamentations provides a window through which to appreciate not only Gene's work to save his family, and in particular, the life of his son, Derek, from drug addiction, but also an open door for the reader to walk through toward self-discovery.

Derek was the pride of his father's heart. In much of his work to save Derek, Gene revealed his own co-dependency. Alcohol and drug addiction are "cunning and baffling" as the big book of

A.A. says. The addict and the co-dependent are confronted with their own powerlessness to get control. Both may be destroyed in the spiral downwards unless spiritual presence and power intervene.

Gene and Derek's story is heartbreaking. But he has given to us a wonderful gift that will promote healing and hope.

As a pastor I have listened many times to parental pain and longsuffering, sometimes ending in rescue, insight, and freedom, but often ending in despair and death for those trapped by the evils of mood-altering chemicals that enslave and slowly destroy. I pray that many will read this book and gain insight that leads to the beginning of recovery, spiritual freedom, and the deepening of forgiving love.

Dr. Jerry Tankersley, Pastor
Laguna Presbyterian Church
Laguna Beach, California

Prologue

The Takeaway I The Comeback

I'd like to share my stories with you, to share with you how life can "take away" but also provide for what I call "the comeback." My own life has been filled with takeaways—failures and losses—and comebacks, or miracles, that have led me to become the fulfilled and grateful man I am today. In spite of the takeaways, my trust and walk with the Lord has always given me the strength and courage to endure and come back. We gain our strength through our weakness, and we build upon it; losses can become wins.

All the events in my life have been the foundation of who I have become. Each takeaway served as a stepping stone to a higher calling and led me to new opportunities that exploited my entrepreneurial skills, gave me confidence to achieve my dreams, led me to loving partners, and allowed me the unparalleled experience of fatherhood.

This growth was augmented by the book *Think and Grow Rich* by Napoleon Hill. The works of this world-famous author inspired me. Og Mandino, like myself, was a byproduct of Napoleon Hill's book. His writings had a profound influence in my business and personal life. I met OG when he was presented the highest honor for the esteemed comeback award called the "Rags to Riches" presented by W. Clement Stone. He had personally experienced a comeback from divorce, drugs, and an attempted suicide at age fifty. His seventeen books sold over one hundred million copies and were translated into ninety-one languages. The photo I took with him still remains in my office. He told me "to love the light, for it shows me the way, yet endure the darkness, for it will always show me the stars." I have always followed Napoleon Hill's creed: "Whatever the mind can conceive and believe, it can achieve." This motto has remained with me my entire life.

The cornerstone of my life, and thus the foundation of my takeaways and comebacks, has always been establishing relationships. I built both professional and social relationships that opened doors of opportunity for me. Relationships take time to develop; they are about allowing people to see and know the real you. Relationships are built upon trust and respect. I learned to listen and understand people's points of view. Over the years, I always went the extra mile to maintain and nurture these relationships.

A book that greatly inspired me in this respect was *Listening with the Third Ear* written by German psychologist Theodore Rike. His premise is that 80% percent of the people you converse with each day never hear or listen or remember what you've said. Another 15% percent don't remember what you've said after forty-eight hours. People who make direct eye contact and look into your eyes are listening and understanding what you are saying with their "third ear."

Now, in my late seventies, I still communicate this way with business associates and friends and maintain strong ties with senior tennis players throughout the U.S. I am deeply involved with my four children and four grandchildren. The woman of my life for nine years has brought me a limitless love and meaning to the depths of my soul.

Relationships are hard to come by, but the relationships that I've built with my children have been the building blocks from which our family could grow and prosper. This has been evident in their lives as adults and parents. Over the years, each has pursued a successful career and returned home for all holidays, special occasions, family reunions, and they have always been there for my partner and me.

I share this background as I highlight the importance of this book: embracing values of family life, in spite of all life's takeaways and comebacks, and demonstrating that each individual's life trajectory is unique. Nowhere was this concept more salient in my life than in my experiences with my son, Derek, who unfortunately battled drug addiction. My son ultimately lost that fight.

As a parent, the loss of my son has been the most devastating experience of my life. It is only now, through my own heart's lamentations, that I have learned to cope, and I wish to bring understanding and insights to others who deal with their children's drug afflictions. My hope is that this book will open your eyes to the takeaways and comebacks in life, and how these, combined with our choices, lead us to our final destination.

Part I

Persecution | Prosperity

The Armenian Genocide

During the Armenian Genocide in 1915, Armenians were deemed expendable by young Turks for their Christian beliefs and were thought to be a threat to the Turkish-Muslim hierarchy.

Talaat Pasha led the systematic extermination of Armenians. He empowered young Turks to go village by village and kill all of the inhabitants. They used extreme means to carry out their crimes: raping women and then stabbing them with swords; stealing their valuables; shooting the men; and in some cases they would march the inhabitants until they starved to death. In all, 1.5 million Armenians were brutally murdered and tortured to death over a period of six months. To this day, the Turkish government denies that the Genocide ever occurred.

Many Armenians, including my grandparents, escaped from Turkey. Those who were fortunate migrated through Ellis Island in New York, and a large group settled in Fresno as early as the 1920's. One of my grandfathers was born in, and escaped from, a village called Kharpet and later, Van. I grew up with the stories of how my grandfather had left behind his home, his land, and everything he owned to escape the horrific killings of the Armenian race.

I have visited Armenia several times, and the scars that remain and lack of recognition by the Turkish government still haunt the Armenian people and the world. On April 24, 2015, Armenians throughout the world recognized and celebrated the one-hundredth anniversary of the Armenian Genocide, with over eight million Armenians living worldwide.

Arnold

My father, Arnold, was born in New Britain, Connecticut in 1906, and he had an older brother, my Uncle Archie. Their mother died when Arnold was two years old. Their father, Martin, my grandfather, also escaped the Genocide. Martin did not speak English, and he decided to marry a relative to help him raise his two boys. With the challenge, or takeaway, of raising two young boys in a non-English-speaking family, they did the best they could to work and make ends meet.

When he was old enough, Arnold worked as a salad chef until he graduated from high school. He then became a waiter, subsequently working at several fine New York restaurants. When he was twenty-seven he had saved enough money to take a vacation to visit his relative, Haigas Bagdasarian, at his ranch in Fowler, California, ten miles south of Fresno, California.

The Bagdasarians were prospering ranchers who grew grapes, peaches, nectarines, figs, and produced grapes for raisins. They were related to the late Ross Bagdasarian, who was better known as David Seville, the creator of the famous Alvin and the Chipmunks. He also wrote the famous song "Come On-A My House" made famous by Rosemary Clooney.

The song became a national hit and can still be heard on radio stations throughout America. The theme epitomizes the love and hospitality of Armenian families throughout the world:

> Come on-a my house, I am going to give you candy,
>
> Come on-a my house, my house I am gonna give you
>
> Apple a plum and apricot–a too eh
>
> Come on-a my house, my house a come on

Come on-a my house, my house a come on

Come on-a my house, my house

I'm gonna give you

Figs and dates and grapes and cakes eh

Come on-a my house, my house a come on,

Come on-a my house, my house a come on,

Come on-a my house, I'm gonna give you candy

Come on-a my house, my house,

I'm gonna give you everything

Come on-a my house, my house, I'm gonna give you
Christmas tree

Come on-a my house, my house, I'm gonna give you

Marriage ring and pomegranate too ah…

Arnold loved Fresno and decided to stay. He began looking for a job.

Elizabeth

My mother, Elizabeth Kalunian, was born in Fresno in 1914 and had two younger sisters. Her father, Sarkis, was fortunate enough to escape Turkey during the Armenian Genocide and migrated to the U.S. He later settled in Sanger, California, a small ranching community east of Fresno.

When Elizabeth was six years old, her family moved to Fresno. They lived on M Street next door to William Saroyan, who went on to become a Pulitzer Prize winner for his books *The Man on the Flying Trapeze* and *My Name is Aram*. William Saroyan was a famous playwright of over three hundred works, including many award-winning plays. He has been enshrined in Fresno where the main performing arts theater is named after him and a full-size statue of him stands in front. Elizabeth would walk to Emerson Elementary School with William each day, and they became close friends.

Elizabeth's mother was eventually diagnosed with tuberculosis and died five months later when Elizabeth was fourteen years old. Elizabeth took over the responsibility of running the family. She raised her two younger sisters and cared for her father who could not read or write, nor could he speak English. However, he had a forty-acre, grape-producing farm in Sanger.

Elizabeth was always groomed conservatively. She had beautiful, black hair, a stunning figure, beautiful skin, stunning facial features, and always had an aura and presence about her. Her eyes glowed with warmth and sincerity. She was called the "Palm Olive girl" for her radiant skin and infectious smile.

Elizabeth became a deep, caring woman who always dressed with taste. She was devoted to her Christian faith and served in the First Armenian Presbyterian Church with her grace and love of God. Elizabeth was a homemaker and made homemade strawberry, apricot, and plum jams. She made Madzoon (Armenian yogurt from scratch), hot and cold dolma, rice pilaf with raisins and pine nuts, Kufta, tabbouleh, kebobs, baklava, and other Armenian delicacies.

They Meet

When Arnold decided to stay in Fresno, a family member introduced him to George Mardikian, an Armenian immigrant from Turkey and founder of the Omar Khayyam's restaurant located in the luxurious Hotel Sequoia in downtown Fresno. Mr. Mardikian hired Arnold as headwaiter, and later as maître d', for his extensive background in the restaurant business. After graduating from Fresno High School, Elizabeth also met George Mardikian, who immediately hired her to work in Omar Khayyam's. The restaurant went on to become one of the most famous in San Francisco history.

Arnold was attracted to Elizabeth and tried on several occasions to have coffee with her. She refused. She was, after all, about to become engaged to an enterprising young man from a very wealthy family. Arnold managed the restaurant employees, and one evening he told Elizabeth she had to help set up the banquet room for a large party the next night and that she would have to do some light painting in the powder room. Elizabeth's trust and innocence opened a door for Arnold. She agreed but eventually realized that this was a ploy to get her attention. At that point, Arnold told her he would do the painting if she would go out and have coffee with him.

There was something special about Arnold. So, after four excruciating months, Elizabeth accepted Arnold's proposal of marriage. I am the result of the persistence of this beautiful marriage that lasted fifty-eight years.

Uncle Archie

My Uncle Archie, my dad's older brother, played a prominent role in the Nalbandian family history.

Archie was three years old when his mother—my grandmother—died. She was twenty years old. An aunt raised Archie and Arnold until they moved to Queens just outside of Manhattan, New York to start their young lives alone.

Archie and Arnold were close, but Archie was more aggressive. He became independent at a very young age. He was very resourceful, had an entrepreneurial spirit that served him well, and had instincts that taught him the art of survival. He always sent money home to his father, Martin, who did not speak English and was unable to work, and cared for his brother, Arnold.

Archie was resourceful. He sold papers, mowed lawns, and did what he needed to do to earn money to support himself. At one point Archie started an egg route and called on families within a five-mile area, and Arnold would deliver the fresh eggs the next day. They became successful, so Archie decided to drop out of school after he finished the eighth grade and move to the Bronx, New York. Arnold stayed behind, as he was only ten years old, while Archie was a mature thirteen.

Archie started another very successful egg route on his bicycle that covered the Bronx, Queens, and parts of Brooklyn. He saw a need for Armenian families who didn't speak English and had trouble communicating; eggs were used for making bread and other Armenian pastries and delicacies. Archie was popular and trusted. He built his business on service and quality. When Archie was making enough money to get a one-bedroom apartment, he called for Arnold to come to New York so they could continue working together.

Archie was a gambler and a risk-taker. He liked playing high-stakes poker games. One night, in a high-stakes game, the pot got very big and the last player to stay in the pot with Archie raised the bet, using his new car as collateral. Archie won the pot and a new $4500 Piece Arrow car.

When Archie won his new car, he began to attract the ladies with his good looks and "affluence." One Sunday afternoon, Archie took his date for a drive in his elegant Pierce Arrow. It was a sleek car with wire wheels, pull-down shades on the windows, and a sliding glass window between the front and back seats with a telephone in the back so the passengers could call the driver. This was Archie's first taste of luxury. Not bad for a seventeen-year-old who had only attended school until the eighth grade.

Archie was driving along a steep street in Queens when suddenly he noticed a tire rolling down the hilly street and said to his date, "Look at that tire rolling down the hill. Some poor guy lost his wheel!" When he came to the stoplight the front end of the car went "clunk" and the right side of the car dropped to the pavement. It was his first lesson in humility and the only date he would have with the young lady.

Archie was a gifted athlete and was picked up by a semi-pro football team. He was the quarterback and field goal kicker. He won the state championship by drop kicking a fifty-yard field goal and was recruited by the Cleveland Browns. He was even better at baseball and was eventually signed as a pitcher with the New York Yankees. Archie went to spring training and played with the legendary King of Swat, Babe Ruth.

Babe Ruth liked Archie for his work ethic. Ruth grew up in an orphanage and virtually raised himself like Archie had. There was a kinship between the two of them that lasted Archie's whole life. The Babe, as he was known, became the most prolific home-run hitter in baseball history, and the famed Yankee Stadium is known today as the house that Ruth built. Ruth was involved in the most memorable baseball trade in the history of baseball. He was a successful pitcher for the Boston Red Sox and was later was traded to the New York Yankees for $125,000. It became known as the worst trade in baseball history, as Ruth eventually led the Yankees to ten World Series wins. This era became legendary in Boston and was immortalized by Bostonians as "The Curse of the Bambino."

Archie was later assigned to play for the Biloxi, a Yankee affiliate in the Southern League, as a young, seventeen-year-old pitcher. Archie had an arm injury that shortened his career. The irony was that his dream and mine were intertwined and led to what defined our destiny.

Upon Archie's return to New York, and at Arnold's request, he came to Fresno for a visit. He fell in love with California. He visited relatives in Los Angeles and decided that it would be his new home. He learned a trade, and at twenty-three years old he started his business, a machine screw company called Yankee Screw Products (an homage to his roots in New York and his beloved Yankees). In this way, Archie's takeaway arm injury in baseball created a comeback.

Archie brought in a partner, John Sarek. They built what became a fifty-year business relationship and a very successful machine shop. John was a master machinist and Archie was adept at forming relationships. With his entrepreneurial skill he brought in major core accounts, namely Douglas Aircraft, Lockheed Aircraft, Emerson TV, Philco-Ford, Raytheon, Whittaker Corp., RCA, and many other blue chip companies. His shop was located in South Central Los Angeles, a crime-driven neighborhood with many poor, African-American families.

Archie's security guard was a schoolteacher named Rufus Jenkins who was respected by the community. Archie would

20

send food to over four hundred African-American families in the area on all holidays and free turkeys every Thanksgiving. He was affectionately known as "Mr. Archie." He was accepted and held in reverence. He was very successful, philanthropic, was a great uncle to my family and me, and a great friend and patron to all who knew him.

Everything Archie achieved was earned. Archie was admired, accepted, and loved. He became a member of the Jockey Club at Santa Anita and Hollywood Parks. He was a 32 degree Mason and later a Shriner, which was a most defining and glorious moment in his life. His close friend, John Forsythe of *Dynasty*, was always with him.

When I was growing up, I was the son that Archie never had. He would ask my dad to let me stay with him and his wife, Marjorie, for a month or so during the summers. I worked in his shop and learned how to set up screw machines and how to assist the high-level machinists, but I would always have an hour-and-a-half-lunch with Archie and Johnny.

Archie was always introducing me to new adventures and interests, including his love of horses. He owned many horses and had a stable at the famed Santa Anita Park in Arcadia. One of his prized horses was Driftin' Along, a two-year-old thoroughbred that had won seven consecutive races and earned a spot to race at the prestigious Kentucky Derby. Three weeks before the Kentucky Derby, Driftin' Along raced at Bay Meadows in San Francisco. During the race he came up lame and had to be scratched from his post at the Kentucky Derby. This was a takeaway that my Uncle Archie was never able to overcome. There were no other "comeback" horses to make up for it, and he always wondered why this great moment was taken from him.

Something that I really enjoyed was that Archie, being the great athlete in the Nalbandian family, always bought me baseball equipment and showed me his memorabilia from when he played in the Yankee organization. He would share his many stories of playing professional baseball. To do what he did became my dream.

George Mardikian

Mr. Mardikian became my godfather when I was born. Throughout my life he inspired me to believe in myself, and he always went the extra mile for people. He was the living example of his beliefs. An immigrant who loved America, he made America a better place to live and would make you proud of your heritage.

Throughout his life, George Mardikian was generous, philanthropic, and was even awarded the Medal of Freedom in 1951 by President Harry Truman. He authored a book of his memories entitled *Song of America* in which he expressed his gratitude for being an American citizen and his hope to build a legacy of success and inspiration for all who knew him. He also served as executive chef under five presidents for state dinners at the White House and went on to found the famous Omar Khayyam's restaurant where my parents met. It was initially located in Fresno, but it was later moved to San Francisco at Taylor and O'Farrell, where dignitaries and people from all walks of life dined for over fifty years.

Mardikian's father was one of two hundred fifty ethnic-Armenian intellectuals and community leaders arrested on April 25, 1915, known as Red Sunday. After the arrest, the Mardikians were driven out of their home and marched to Erzincan. His

22

grandmother committed suicide by jumping into the Euphrates River while the rest of the family was beaten to death or burned alive.

Having witnessed the massacre of his mother's side of the family, George wanted to avenge their deaths and prove to his mother how much of a warrior he was. As a result of his ambition, Mardikian ran away from his home and joined the Armenian volunteer units, in which his Uncle Krikor was a high-ranking member. After World War I ended, George returned to his home where he was a war hero. He arrived at Ellis Island on July 22, 1922. He went to San Francisco and later moved to Fresno, California and opened Omar Khayyam's lunch counter. He was an immediate success. Even through the Depression, people poured into his restaurant to enjoy his famous clam chowder, chili con carne, and pot roast.

He inspired me as a young Armenian boy by instilling in me the belief that I could accomplish my dreams by believing in myself. He always said that he was the luckiest man alive. I learned from him that the real gift in life was not what we receive but what we give of ourselves.

Later on in my own life, when I was hired as president and CEO of Blum's, I went to San Francisco where then-mayor Joseph Alioto and legendary department store retailer, Cyril Magnin—who became a friend and mentor—gave me the key to the city. I received an immediate call from Mr. Mardikian's secretary inviting my wife and me for dinner at his restaurant. He had arranged a special dinner to honor me and introduce me to all his esteemed customers, letting them know of my appointment and—most importantly—that I was his godson.

Part II

Humble Beginnings I Pursuing the Dream

Childhood

Born to Armenian parents in 1937, I grew up in Fresno California in the center of the Central Valley where agriculture was the engine that drove the economy.

My sister, Barbara, was born in 1940. Our lives were simple, and we moved every year until I was six years old. My mother stayed home to care for my sister and me, and my father rode his bike to work at the PG&E offices in downtown Fresno. My parents were loving people. Each Sunday we would attend Sunday school and church at the First Armenian Presbyterian Church located on First and Huntington Avenues. My mom was very active in the Women's League and her beloved Fidelis Club, and would cook for the annual church bazaar each year. My dad was active in local affairs. He became president of the Armenian Citizens League for the San Joaquin Valley and was very well-respected by his peers. He later became president of the Fresno Rotary Club.

Barbara and I were blessed to have our parents' brothers and sisters in our lives. My mom had two sisters, Gladys and Nevart, and two half-brothers—Levon Zakarian, a college professor at Hills College in San Francisco, and Crosby Shapazian, a charismatic farmer who owned two hundred acres in Dinuba, a rich agricultural farming area south of Fresno. Our aunts were always there for us. They made sure we had what we needed in the way of school clothes and that we had special gifts for holidays and birthdays.

Uncle Levon was always dressed in a suit and tie and wore a fedora. He stressed to me the importance of academics and going to college. He taught me to read books and learn vocabulary. I admired him and was deeply influenced by his concern for me. Partly as a result of his influence, I was the first in the Nalbandian family to attend and graduate from college

When I was eight years old I worked with my cousin, Crosby, on his ranch during the summer. That is where I learned how to pick fruit, tomatoes, and grapes. I learned to drive a tractor and worked in the packing house where all the fruit was packed and shipped to his customers. I always enjoyed going to lunch with Crosby, as he was very popular with all the farmers in the surrounding area—Visalia, Orosi, Yettem, and Kingsburg. I learned to hunt and shoot my Daisy BB gun, and I swam daily in Crosby's big irrigation reservoir. He was always there for our family and would bring fruit and vegetables during rough times. My Aunt Margaret would always prepare Armenian dinners during my stays and is still beautiful today at ninety-five years old. It is always a joy to go home, visit her at her home in Bakersfield, and reminisce about my days growing up and living on the ranch.

At that time my family did not have nearly what we have today in terms of money or resources. We learned to work for everything we wanted and needed. My mother did all the washing by hand and hung the clothes to dry. She scrubbed the floors, ironed our clothes, made homemade jams, and always made us look presentable.

College Years

I graduated from Roosevelt High School and played baseball for legendary high school coach Ollie Bidwell. We won the Central Valley Baseball Championship in 1955, led by my close friend, Kalem Barserian, at the Sam Lynn Park in Bakersfield, California.

During my high school years I played against great major league pitchers born and raised in Fresno: Jim Maloney of the Cincinnati Reds, Dick Ellsworth of the Chicago Cubs, Lynn Ruby of the St. Louis Cardinals, and Dick Selma of the New York Mets. Other pitchers in college were Truman Clevenger of the New York Yankees and Jack Hannah of the Milwaukee Braves, who became the best high school baseball coach at Bullard High School and the Central Valley, and is now a gospel country music star affectionately known as the "Singing Cowboy."

Fresno is known for producing great athletes in all sports from high school and college. Fresno State is always nationally ranked as one of the top ten baseball schools in the U.S. Other notable major league pitchers from Fresno were Ewell "The Whip" Blackwell and Hall of Famer Tom Seaver of the New York Mets.

Fresno is located in the central part of California and is known as the raisin capital of the world. The Central Valley is the number-one agricultural region in the world, beginning in the northern part of the state in the capital city of Sacramento and stretching far south to Bakersfield. The Valley is prolific in producing numerous varieties of grapes, raisins, all varieties of fresh vegetables and fruits such as apricots, plums, nectarines, peaches, and cantaloupes, and is most famous for its almonds, walnuts, and figs.

After graduating from high school I went to the powerful baseball school, Fresno State, on a baseball scholarship and played for legendary baseball coach Pete Beiden. In 1958 our team went to the College World Series. Another takeaway came

27

when I was declared academically ineligible by one grade point and was unable to play. My comeback however, came when I graduated and pitched in the AABC baseball playoff game, struck out twenty batters, and was signed by one of the great baseball scouts, Gene Handley, of the Chicago Cubs in 1962. It was my boyhood dream. I became an instant celebrity and played with my childhood heroes and great stars, including Ernie "Let's Play Two" Banks, Lou Brock, Ron Santo, and the late Kenny Hubbs. I was living the dream I had always believed in.

Sadly, though, toward the end of spring training I tore the bursa sac in my right shoulder and was devastated to learn I could not pitch again. It was a crushing takeaway in my life, representing a dream that would never be fulfilled.

After pondering this takeaway, I decided to move to Los Angeles, where a comeback came in the form of admission to the UCLA business school MBA program. While attending I was hired as the varsity pitching coach by UCLA baseball coach Art Reichle. I coached some of the greatest players to graduate from UCLA: all-American and Olympic champion Keith Erickson, all-American basketball player Gail Goodrich, and all-American Walt Hazzard. During this time I was privileged to know, work with, and learn from the greatest coach in college sports, a devout Christian named John Wooden, whom we warmly addressed as "Coach." His book *Pyramid of Success* has been by revered by CEO's, coaches, the sports public, teachers, pastors, authors, poets, and children whose parents used Coach Wooden as an example of humility and faith in God.

I continued my studies and earned my MBA degree with honors. It was a glorious moment for my mom and dad and family. The road to earning my MBA from one of the finest business schools in the country was significant. It was the result of what I had learned in my early years: hard work, believing in yourself, and staying persistent will make your dreams come to pass.

Faith

While in college I became a born-again Christian at a Billy Graham crusade in Fresno. While I was finishing my graduate studies, I was introduced to Henrietta Mears, a most remarkable woman, who founded Gospel Light Press. She has prepared some of our greatest pastors the world over for the ministry through her inspiring and faith-filled life. Some of these Christian leaders whose reach was worldwide include Dr. Louis Evans, Dr. Ray Lindquist, Dr. Lloyd Ogilvie, Rev. Donn Moomaw, and Dr. William "Bill" Bright. In fact, while attending UCLA I had the opportunity to meet Bill Bright, the founder of Campus Crusade for Christ. He asked me to speak to college fraternities alongside Olympian decathlon champion Rafer Johnson about our faith.

Using my "celebrity" status, I became an integral part of Henrietta Mears' Hollywood Presbyterian Church, which boasted a church membership of over ten thousand congregants. I also became involved with the church collegiate group that had over two thousand students from all over Southern California. She challenged me to go to Guatemala as part of an outreach team and work with the Mayan Indians and their fifty-three different tribunals. I agreed.

During my time in Guatemala I experienced culture shock. It was an impoverished, pagan culture in which there were witch doctors and people were surrounded by a fear of sorcery. It affected my life profoundly. After returning I initially felt a calling to go into the ministry and attend Princeton University. Later, however, after meeting with Ms. Mears and Bill Bright, I told them that I could no longer use my perceived celebrity status; I felt like an actor telling people about my faith when in reality I lacked the Christian maturity to lead and influence groups. It was a moment of truth that awakened me to the truth about myself.

Post-College Pursuits

After completing my MBA I was recommended for a job at UCLA and hired by Chancellor Franklin Murphy as his special assistant for public affairs and university relations. Knowing of my Armenian ethnicity and the history of the Genocide, he told me to reach out to the Armenian community. If I could raise two million dollars, the Regents of California would match the money and endow a chair of Armenian studies at UCLA with three professors. It was my first opportunity to reach out to the American community and travel around the United States.

I met with many successful Armenians who had immigrated from Turkey and Armenia before and during the Genocide to find prosperity and a good life. They sought freedom from persecution of the Turkish regime through hard work and their Christian faith. (The Armenians were the first to adopt Christianity as their religion in 301 A.D. They also introduced architecture to the world.)

After asking for money during twelve thousand miles of travel, I encountered some resistance. They questioned me about my religious beliefs and my politics. Most of the individuals were not highly educated, but they had succeeded through hard work and giving back to the community. I was fortunate enough to meet one of the most remarkable, self-made, distinguished immigrants from Armenia. He founded and built the New York Stock Exchange corporation named Masco. His name was Alex Manoogian.

I was invited to meet him at his world headquarters in the Buhl Building in Detroit, Michigan. We had lunch and a two-hour meeting. He asked if I could stay another day, which I did. Alex drove me around and showed me the Gold Dome Church that he had built outside of Detroit and his sprawling estate that he had donated to the city for the mayor's residence. He was essentially the patriarch of the Armenian people in today's society. Alex was later the silent force in completing one of the greatest gifts for the Armenian community—the Armenian Library for UCLA.

I was at a crossroads, faced with the task of trying to raise two million dollars. I had had no takers after my first tour. Some donors asked me what they would get out of the deal if they donated. My only answer was, "We will preserve and create awareness of our wonderful and faith-filled history."

Coming from a modest background, I had witnessed the success of many Armenians in the field of agriculture in the San Joaquin Valley. They took pride in showing their wealth. Therefore, I decided to host a gala dinner and rent the ballroom of the Beverly Hilton Hotel for over one thousand people. This event was to preserve and bring awareness to the history of the Armenian race.

I worked on getting a headliner and was turned down by Bob Hope and Johnny Carson, but I was able to book Danny Thomas. I had the tickets printed three months in advance and invited notable politicians, entertainers, local businesspeople, and of course, Dr. Murphy. We sold out within two weeks, with 70% of the Armenian community attending.

The night before the event I called Mr. Thomas' office and spoke with Barbara to confirm the location of where Danny would meet me for a private cocktail party with some of the big donors I had lined up. Then it happened: I was blindsided when she told me that Danny was starring at the Sands Hotel in Las Vegas for the next two weeks and would not be able to attend my event. She said she was sorry and that they would send a private donation. This happened in the early afternoon a day before the event.

Desperately I took a deep breath. Then it came to me to call him directly, which I did. I called his room at the Sands and a woman picked up the phone. I told her who I was and said that Danny was the headliner for the Armenian Endowment fundraiser dinner at the Beverly Hills Hilton the following evening. She said she was sorry but explained that Danny was appearing twice nightly at the Sands. She said they would send a donation to support the cause.

I sat in my office at UCLA, and at 6:45 p.m., less than twenty-four hours before the event, I deviously called Danny's room. Again a woman answered the phone. I disguised my voice and told her that Dr. Murphy from UCLA was calling. I heard her whisper to Danny. The next thing I heard was Danny's voice on the other end. Taking a deep breath, I told him I was Gene Nalbandian and I was calling for Dr. Murphy. I told him I had booked this event four months prior and he was expected as the headliner for over one thousand people. He told me that he, too, was sorry but that he would send a donation.

I went on to tell him that the Armenians were coming to the event because they thought he was Armenian. He responded that the Jews thought he was Jewish, too. We laughed and he said he had to go. I told him I had a deal to offer: I would guarantee him fifty thousand dollars for the evening. After a big pause he said to hold on for a moment. When he came back on the line, he said, "Gene, I will do this and attend on one condition." I was prepared to lose money covering the costs of putting on this banquet when he said, "I will come if you allow me to bring my Las Vegas show ensemble with Sergio Franchi."

"We have a deal!" I replied immediately.

He interrupted. "Gene, this will be my donation to your cause and your contagious spirit."

Danny arrived at the cocktail party with dignitaries and the press, and during his set he had the audience in the palm of his hand. He described his struggles as a young man growing up in poverty, but his love of family and ethnicity gave him the foundation and basis to reach his life's dream. We hugged after the event, took pictures, and I thanked him sincerely. He said, "You gave me something tonight, Gene. Always remember to give back."

That evening we raised a little over two million dollars, largely based on Danny's passion, love of family, and his pride in being Lebanese, which is similar to the Armenian culture. It was a great moment.

All was well. The endowment of the Armenian chair went on to receive national attention, and I received letters and acknowledgments for my accomplishments. I felt that I had gone above and beyond to get the job done. The Armenian chair was also later established at the University of California, Berkeley campus, and both UCB and UCLA now offer graduate programs in Armenian studies.

After the success of the Armenian Endowment fundraiser, I got a call from Dr. Murphy. He told me that there was an incredibly rare collection of books that represented the largest library of the history of the Armenian race. It was available if we could raise 2.5 million dollars in forty-eight hours. I couldn't use the money raised at the banquet, and I knew only one person who could help. I made the call to Alex Manoogian. He asked the name of the collection and said he would be on the next plane from Detroit to Los Angeles. I picked him up at LAX airport and we had a private lunch with Dr. Murphy in his office. After lunch, Mr. Manoogian gave the greatest gift to the Armenian chair, which was the acquisition of the rarest collections of books of Armenian history and the origins of its evolution by writing a check for the entire amount and donating the collection to the UCLA Library, which now houses one of the largest collections of rare books in the world.

To my surprise, and to the surprise of the UCLA community, Dr. Murphy announced his resignation. The individual who had helped shape UCLA's medical school into one of the finest institutions in the world was leaving the university to become the chairman and CEO of the L.A. Times. Before leaving he told me I could join him in a similar role there with a good salary. However, I was at a point in my life where I wanted to be my own man and pursue my dream of owning and building my own business.

Part III

Divorce I Custody

Marriage and Divorce

Upon the completion of my six-month mission to Guatemala, I was asked to speak before the congregation at Hollywood Presbyterian Church. After services, a church greeter (an attractive woman) said my message inspired her. She touched my heart. She was valedictorian of her high school class and a graduate of Bob Jones University, and her parents had also been missionaries in Cuba for fourteen years. I felt that our faith together could accomplish great things.

After I graduated from college, we married. She had a young daughter with whom I fell in love, and I immediately adopted her. We also had two sons together—Stephan and Jon David. However, after six and a half years, in the midst of seven years of personal, financial, and business success, my wife and I could not reconcile our ongoing differences, and our marriage was taken away in divorce. At the same time, I was coming upon trying times with my business partner, having experienced philosophical differences and the sale of our company.

The divorce consumed me. My dear mother had been calling every day, begging me to get custody of the children. It was a strain on me. My mother was very tenacious and a good mother, so she could not comprehend not having the children in our family.

In spite of these overwhelming and difficult takeaways, my comeback came in the form of a landmark custody case in 1972: I was the first father in San Francisco County to be awarded full, permanent custody of his children. I was granted custody of our two boys, and three months later, full custody of our daughter, Michelle. At the time, Jon David was eleven months old, Stephan was three, and Michelle was turning six.

Dad Life

When I was awarded custody of my three children, my life was focused on establishing a foundation for them. Nothing more mattered to me.

As parents we all wish to live a full life watching each of our children grow up, get their primary education, go on to college, graduate, get a job, and support themselves (what a great day that is!), get married, have children, and then we get to be grandparents. The trials and tribulations of raising our children are opportunities for us to learn and grow from each experience and to mature in the process.

Having had five children through two marriages was a big challenge for me as a young Armenian-American father who grew up in a loving family with parents who had no formal education. I became a full-time mom and dad for eight years raising Jon David, Stephan, and Michelle. It takes real entrepreneurial skills to do the job of raising three children. I integrated my Armenian upbringing into the way I ran my home, having the organizational skills to make it all work. Being organized meant cooking three meals a day, changing diapers, potty training, washing and ironing clothes, giving nightly baths, reading bedtime stories, making beds, and maintaining a clean and orderly house.

I'd prepare all meals in advance so I could spend time with the children. At each meal we would have prayers of thanksgiving, and in the evenings after dinner, instead of watching TV, Steve and Michelle would stand up for thirty minutes and discuss what they were learning in school and what experiences were beneficial to their personal development. Each month they would also write a book report and we would discuss it after dinner. This was how I began to teach them to think on their feet.

I did my best to create an environment of accountability. Each child was assigned to daily chores—making their bed, brushing their teeth, cleaning the dining table after meals, emptying the trash, and completing their homework. I made a scoreboard and awarded colored stars that denoted the degree of their accomplishments each day. A total score was given at the end of the week, which resulted in a monetary reward that could be invested, saved, or a portion of which could be spent on something they wanted. Watching TV was also earned on the star system, and viewing was used for educational growth.

For ten years we lived in our three-bedroom loft in beautiful San Francisco. I planned activities for the children on the weekends. We would visit the famous Flashacker Zoo, go to museums, enjoy lunch at Fisherman's Wharf, attend Giants baseball games, go fishing every Sunday in Sausalito, and spend a lot of time at Golden Gate Park (the equivalent to Central Park in New York).

During this time, the late seventies, there was racial tension throughout the Bay Area. Haight-Ashbury in particular was the home of the Hippie and Free Speech Movements, of Timothy O' Leary and his LSD and ESP movements. LSD, marijuana, and heroin were part of this Free Love Movement. It was a time where drugs were used to escape responsibility and accountability for one's actions.

Every child was bussed outside their district, and Steve and Michelle were bussed to the controversial Haight-Ashbury Elementary School, which was guarded by twenty uniformed policemen. They were integrated into classrooms with poverty-stricken children from low-income African-American families, as mandated by the law to try to overcome racial tension with the objective of preserving human rights and equality.

During this time I educated my children on the use of drugs and how harmful they were to their minds and bodies, that drug use would lead to a world of darkness without light. Little did I know that drug abuse would become central in my life later on.

Being a single dad had its advantages. After Stephan and Michelle were bussed off to school each morning, I took Jon David to Golden Gate Park to pet the animals and ride the swings and go down the slides. All the mothers with small children would meet at the park and we would discuss everything from parenting, new recipes, and everything related to their marriages. Each day they would anticipate my arrival and ask me questions about how I was able to be a single parent and do all the chores that moms do every day. They would ask me what I liked to cook, and I would share some of my Armenian recipes. They wanted to know my philosophy on raising children and if I would remarry. They would always tell me that their husbands could never do what I was doing.

I would invite the children's friends over to share and play games. We would take walks to the park together, tell stories, and do things that would build trust and respect for one another. I would also invite their friends' parents over to our home in order to build relationships, and they would reciprocate.

After four years I was running out of money and did odd jobs, but I still had to be home in time to be with the children when they returned home from school. It seemed like a burden, but it was an experience that gave me the determination that I could start and run my own businesses. That was to come.

Part IV

Discouraging Failures I Unexpected Success

Entrepreneurial Beginnings

Somewhere along the line, I learned that an entrepreneur is "one who finds a need and fills it." Growing up, I sensed the struggle to make ends meet, so when I was sixteen years old I took my first step toward becoming an entrepreneur (though at the time I did not know what that meant). In the summer of 1953, my close friend, Richard "Butch" Lang, and I discovered a need for debeaking turkeys in the community and went out to fill it.

The San Joaquin Valley raises over 700,000 turkeys a year. When young turkeys are two weeks old they must be vaccinated and debeaked to prevent them from pecking each other to death and to enable them to eat with ease.

Butch and I developed a machine with a heated blade and a wire connected to a pedal that moved down onto a steel rod that would cut the beak off and cauterize the vein so the bird would not bleed to death. It was a captive market. We earned $0.015 per bird and earned over five hundred dollars a week for a period of fourteen weeks, working twelve hours a day during the summer nights.

As a result of our hard work, I was able to purchase a new 1956 Chevy Bel Air for my dad since we did not have a family car. It was such a joyous and happy time for my dad, as he was now able to ride to work in a new car. Plus, I was able to use the car on the weekends. It was the beginning of what was to become the start of my entrepreneurial life.

Business Endeavors

Blum's

Upon his resignation, Dr. Murphy kindly made a call to Walter

Candy, chairman of the prestigious department store Bullock's. I was hired as a buyer, and after two years I became a merchandise manager. When Bullock's merged with Federated, I sought a better experience. I was subsequently hired by KMPG (Peat, Marwick & Mitchell) as a senior consultant and was given my first assignment: working with Polly Bergen, whose company was going public, introducing her famous Turtle of the Oil line of cosmetics.

We had a successful launch. Through my department store knowledge and experience I was able to get her line in over one hundred of the most prestigious department stores in the country. She asked me, as part of my assignment, to find her a president and CEO for her company. I lined up four top executives for her consideration. After a month-long search, Polly and her top advisor, Ralph Lewis, told me they wanted me as their president.

When I told the managing partner at KMPG, I was immediately fired for using the firm to further my own interests. Though that wasn't the case, I got trapped in the politics of a big company and became a scapegoat. I reluctantly got legal counsel and was going to press charges when the managing partner told me I could stay but would have to find another job or leave within six months.

After an exhausting job search I finally found a job. I would be heading up the 100-year-old prestigious candy, confectionery, and popular restaurant company Blum's of San Francisco, part of a public company named NATEC that had ten subsidiaries. At twenty-nine years old I was hired as their president and CEO. I turned out to be one of the youngest presidents in the country with eventual sales that totaled over ten million dollars. I became an instant member of YPO, the Young Presidents

Organization, and I had the honor of working with some of the top CEO's in the country.

Within two years we virtually doubled sales through a national marketing campaign during which I personally went to all the major department stores, negotiated real estate, built a cable car theme for candy sales, and filled our first store in conjunction with Marvin Traub, CEO and chairman of Bloomingdales. New Yorkers loved our product. The unique packaging and department layout helped increase their candy sales 100%.

I had the occasion to meet with one of the most prestigious retail pioneers, esteemed retailer Stanley Marcus, founder of Neiman Marcus, in the famous Zodiac Room in Dallas. Together we expanded our line of products to the Neiman Marcus chain with record sales. Other great retailers I dealt with, and subsequently established a presence in their stores, included Marshall Field's, Chicago, Wanamaker's, Philadelphia, Joske's, Houston, and Rich's Atlanta, among others.

One day I got a call from Mr. Ben Cohen, president of the famous and luxurious Fontainebleau Hotel in Miami Beach. He wanted a big cable car in his lobby, which we built, and it became such a success that he wanted our Blum's restaurant to be a part of his famous hotel. The famous Fairmont, owned by a giant in the hotel industry and my future mentor, Benjamin Swig, had a Blum's restaurant, and we doubled sales through a program Mr. Swig and I developed. The five-star hotel was a landmark in San Francisco at the top of Nob Hill and boasted guests including U.S. Presidents, CEO's, U.S. senators, movie stars, and other people of fame and fortune. Mr. Swig sent a list of all his guests each week, and I developed for each a box of our finest chocolates, designed by merchandise manager Wanda Myers, called Blum's President Box.

At the end of my third year as CEO, I was recognized at the Balboa Bay Club in Newport Beach on December 22, 1971 as outstanding president of our ten divisions, and I was elected to the board of directors.

Nine days later, however, a big takeaway caught me off guard. I was fired by the chairman of our parent company for casting a vote against a policy change he wanted to make. I was devastated and did not know where to turn. I was out of a job with three children and no income. It was then that I was destined to start and run my own company.

Luigi's

I called Ben Swig and he invited me to his office. In a tearful state I told him I had just been fired and had three kids to support. He slammed his fist down on his large mahogany table and said, "Young man, you have been privileged." He explained that when he was thirty-eight years old he went bankrupt for the third time. He said there was only one other person who had had more bankruptcies than him—and that person's name was Hilton.

A few weeks later, I got a call from the attorney for the fifty-five Luigi's restaurants in San Francisco. He wanted to set up a meeting with Mr. Louis Perini, the owner of a mega-construction and development company in Boston and owner of the National League baseball team the Boston Braves.

Mr. Perini said his fifty-five restaurants were not doing well, and he asked me, as the former CEO of Blum's, what I would do to fix the problem and prevent bankruptcy. I told him his stores were not clean, the food presentation was inconsistent, and his take-out business was hurting him. The stores needed to concentrate on customer service. After an hour-long meeting he told me he wanted to hire me.

He asked what I wanted in salary. With my leg shaking under the table, I mustered all my fortitude and confidence and told him $10,000 a month. I thought he was going to go ballistic. His response was, "Who the hell do you think I am?" I told him politely that if he wanted the job done, that would be my price. His attorney and several board members were present, and he wanted to have a one-hour meeting with them. They returned shortly and welcomed me to the company. I also received health insurance and an office space in one of his prestigious buildings in downtown San Francisco.

I turned the company around after a year to the delight of Mr. Perini. He was able to sell the chain at a profit. He was grateful and gave me a gift.

Swensen's

I was out of a job again, but I had saved a good amount of money. At that point I was called upon by the attorney who owned the franchise rights to Swensen's Ice Cream, a company with two locations in San Francisco and a couple small stores outside the city.

William Meyer, a promoter in the entertainment business, and I bought the rights to Swensen's and had the privilege of bringing on the creator of this wonderful ice cream, Earle Swensen, a former policeman in San Francisco who had a shop that became one of the twenty official landmarks in the City by the Bay located at Union and Hyde Streets on the cable car route to Fisherman's Wharf.

Just about everyone in the world travels to San Francisco at some point and remembers the famous song by Tony Bennett "I Left My Heart in San Francisco." Therefore, Bill and I created a memorable new motif around the city. People came for the decor and to be served award-winning ice cream in beautiful glassware. We were going up against Baskin Robbins, which had over seven hundred stores with average annual sales of $250,000 to $300,000.

We opened our first new store right off the UCLA campus, which generated 1.8 million dollars in the first year. In year one in the Beverly Hills location we generated 2.5 million with big-name movie stars as customers.

I got a call that MGM Grand in Las Vegas wanted a full-service Swensen's as well. This location generated an unbelievable 4.5 million dollars the first year and is still going strong. We were written up in all the major magazines—*Forbes*, *Business Week*, the *Wall Street Journal*, and *Fortune*. Then, during the "LUV" craze in America, we came out with a new flavor called "love," and our slogan became, "We make love and other flavors, too." The slogan went viral. We were interviewed on radio and TV shows, and our business took off like a rocket ship.

I went on to buy a construction company whose owner was a friend, and we built over fourteen hundred stores in a period of six years. We were located in every major metropolitan city throughout the U.S. We were doing so well that Bill bought a used Cadillac and hired a chauffeur, James Roosevelt, who drove us everywhere, including important meetings and high-level social events in San Francisco. Bill brought in another partner, however, which created a conflict during my divorce. I chose to leave the company and took the responsibility of raising my three young children as a single parent. A year later Bill sold Swensen's when it was at the top, but for me it wasn't about money; it was about raising my young children.

Entrepreneurial Endeavors

It was through the disciplined process of raising my three kids that I was later able to build financially successful companies.

Tweezer Lite

After raising my children for eight years as a single parent, I started a cosmetic company called Tweezer Lite. I had invented a cosmetic tweezer with surgical, stainless-steel blades and a built-in light for tweezing eyebrows and removing splinters. The company did well selling to major department stores and high-end drug store chains. I held two patents that both were featured on the cover of the Sears catalog.

My Uncle Archie's company manufactured and assembled the Tweezer Lite and my company did the packaging and distribution to all the major department stores in the U.S. These stores included Bloomingdale's, Neiman Marcus, Bullocks, Wanamaker's, Marshall Field's, Sanger Harris, Burdines's, J.L. Hudson's, and over one hundred other major stores. Later I modified the casing to a colorful plastic and sold to all the major drug store chains in the U.S. such as Walgreens, Rite Aid, Thrifty Drug, People's Drug, Fred Meyer, CVS, Echard's, Sears, and other leading drug chains with health and beauty aid departments.

The Tweezer Lite was the feature item in the 1979-1980 Sears catalog and recorded the fourth highest sales in that Christmas season. I made and ran television ads in the major markets and generated record sales for our burgeoning company.

My bank had given me a large line of credit, so I was able to expand my business six-fold. A major cosmetic company approached me after eight years of business to buy my company. They were listed on the New York Stock Exchange. The offer was cash plus stock. The negotiations were intense and demanded my time, which ran up legal and accounting fees. The deal was in escrow, but the day before closing the company controller called me and said the deal was off due to a company crisis and cash flow problems. The deal had consumed me for six weeks and I had spent large sums of money that drained the company's cash advance from my bank. It was a huge takeaway.

My bank then called my loan, as I had leveraged my line of credit to expand my business. When the deal did not go through as planned, I wound up closing my business and mortgaged my home to pay off the loan. Entrepreneurs learn that takeaways are inevitable in business, but it is eternally important to persevere and find a way to come back.

Once again I was faced with no income and raising a family of five. I took six months off, and used what remaining equity I had, to take a time out to understand why things happened and to deal with this loss and apparent failure.

All this adds up to taking the next step and believing in yourself; ideas come to those whose experiences have taught them that all things are possible to those who believe in God (Mark 9:23). It was the beginning of patenting an idea of what is now the subirrigation growing system. It is common knowledge that 96% of all patents issued are not realized because of lack of capital or an inner lack of confidence. My first of three patents through Knobbe, Baer, Olsen & Martens cost $60,000 and became so successful that two major corporations tried to copy my invention. However, they failed after two years, as the key to any patent is your "trade secrets" that set you apart.

Subsurface Irrigation System

Jardinier

The patented subsurface irrigation system that I developed would change the course of the foliage-growing industry and the billion-dollar interior plantscape industry of which Jardinier became the leader. My growing system was designed with a built-in drain system that allowed water to be drawn from the built-in reservoir through capillary action.

My first step was to build prototypes and have each grow system tested by Dr. Wesley Jarrell, professor of soil science at the University of California at Riverside. After a year of testing, the results were astounding, and Dr. Jarrell published a major article denoting the system's merits that would bring economies, conservation, and ecology to this emerging market.

The first company to learn of the subirrigation growing system was Nordstrom department stores. They immediately tested the growing system and wanted to order five thousand systems for the opening of their Brea, California store. I had not completed the tooling and was raising monies to complete the investment of $700,000 to build the molds. Several months later I received another call from Nordstrom's as they were opening their largest store at the Pentagon Mall in Washington, D.C. and gave me an opening order of $250,000.

It was a bittersweet moment; I still did not have credit as my molder wanted 50% down. I called Nordstrom's back in dismay and the secretary said I would be receiving a reply via mail. To my surprise, the next day I received an overnighted and certified letter with a certified check for $250,000 signed by company CEO John Nordstrom with a note saying, "Gene, I trust this gets our order and delivery on time for our store opening. Best of Luck, John Nordstrom."

It was the beginning of branding my company, Jardinier, and the subirrigation containers (systems) were installed in all the one hundred-plus Nordstrom stores throughout the United States for its water conservation, labor saving, and what John Nordstrom claimed to be ecologic (eco)/system, which became a key profit center for maintaining all their foliage in their interior and exterior landscapes.

We formed a University of Nordstrom's in which I taught all the personnel how to use and install our subirrigation systems that provided labor-saving economies, virtually zero plant loss, no overwatering, and brought clean air to the environment, as our systems maintained healthy plants that metabolized all the pollutants in the stores and produced clean air (oxygen). Our maintenance system became a profit center for Nordstrom and was a model for what was to come.

Through the Nordstrom experience I was led to Bill Evans, the chief landscape architect and overseer for the Walt Disney Corporation's interior and exterior landscapes for their hotels and theme parks in Orlando and Anaheim. The Jardinier system was implemented in all Disney properties for water conservation, eliminating overwatering and water runoff, labor saving, and the ecologic benefits of cleaning and metabolizing all pollutants in the air. Our system led to the Clean Act legislation through the research and development studies of three major universities and companies.

Hyatt landscape architect Lee Ackman, with CEO Darryl Leonard, incorporated the Jardinier systems throughout all the

Park Hyatt, Hyatt Regency, Hyatt Resorts, and Grand Hyatt hotels in the U.S. Again, the economies and water conservation of the patented system became standard throughout Hyatt hotels, which led us to the JW Marriott Corporation. Jardinier became the economic engine through its patented technology, which led to our acquisition of a high-quality, decorative container company into which each Jardinier system would fit to allow the landscape maintenance companies to water once every three to four weeks instead of watering once or twice a week. The Jardinier system became the standard for the 6200 interior landscape maintenance companies throughout the U.S., as it reduced labor costs, prevented overwatering, and reduced plant replacement costs by 40%.

I had organized over twenty-five of the top growers in South Florida to begin growing all their foliage in the Jardinier system. After one year the foliage grew lush, cutting the growing cycle by six months, and up to eighteen months for Kentia Palms. It was then that I branded our product "Jardinier Grown Foliage" and began selling our concept directly to major hotel chains, amusement parks, and convention centers. The biggest customers became the 6200 interior plantscape companies throughout the U.S. The growing system cut watering and maintenance costs by 50% and became the number-one foliage growing system in the country.

On the heels of a devastating takeaway, a messy divorce from my wife of twenty-seven years, a real comeback came when a New York investment group liked Jardinier and my three water conservation and water runoff patents. They said they wanted to take the company through a public offering by selling its stock and that I would receive 46% of the stock, becoming the largest shareholder of the public company. An energy—a purpose, a transformation—came over me. Creating strategies to position our new company for the public offering launch was exhilarating and magical, but it took a heavy toll on my time.

David (Top 5 ATP World Tennis player) and
Gene (Top 5 USTA senior doubles during 2000-2006)

Nalbandian Signs Chicub Bonus Contract

Gene Nalbandian, former Roosevelt High School and Fresno State Colelge athlete, has signed a contract with the Chicago Cubs of the National League and will report to Mesa, Ariz., for spring training and assignment March 12th.

Nalbandian, who played the outfield and first base during his prep and collegiate career, was signed to a bonus contract by Gene Hadley, west coast supervisor for the Cubs, as a pitcher.

He was recommended by former Cubs catcher Dutch Seebold, who watched him perform during the Porterville semi professional tournament last Summer.

FRESNAN SIGNS — Gene Nalbandian, center,

Gene signing baseball contract
with chief scout Gene Handley

Elizabeth with Gene at birth

Gene warming up before ballgame

Gene, one year old, with Elizabeth

Derek, eight years old

Elizabeth and Arnold

Nalbandian family photo: Gene,
sister Barbara, Elizabeth, and Arnold

Gene, Danny Thomas, Dr. Franklin Murphy, John Conte (actor),
and George Deukmejian (later California Governor)

Arnold and Elizabeth celebrating fifty years of marriage

Gene, representing the USA at opening of the ATP World Senior
Double Championships 2000 in Australia

Armenian Hall of Famers inducted in Los Angeles:
Harry Hugasian (Stanford), Sam Boghosian (two Super Bowl wins),
Chuck Essegian (All-American, Stanford, and World Series hero,
L.A. Dodgers 1959), and Gene Nalbandian
(UCLA coach, baseball, and top senior tennis doubles)

Derek, nine years old with Dad

Uncle Archie

Gene and Derek

Gene, California House Speaker Jesse Unruh,
Assemblyman Walter J. Karabian, and
Donald Livingston, Cabinet Secretary to Governor Reagan

Bottom Row: David Hedison (actor),
UCLA Chancellor Dr. Franklin Murphy, Mike Connors (actor,
Mannix) Back Row: Larry Balakian (businessman), and Gene

Gene, Arshag Dikranian (philanthropist), and
California Governor Ronald Reagan

Gene and Dr. Murphy

Part V

A Son's Struggles | A Son's Spirit

In the Beginning

One day, while I was immersed in business with my Tweezer Lite cosmetic company, the managing partner of my ad agency told me he wanted me to meet a lovely single woman for a blind date. She was a charming woman fifteen years younger than me. That was a concern, but my children adored her and benefited from her maternal traits. We married a year later and had two children, Jeanne and Derek.

Derek was born in 1980 at Hoag Presbyterian Hospital in Newport Beach, California. He was a handsome boy with a perpetual smile and a big heart full of love, a boy that any father would be proud of. When he was eight days old, my wife and I were having lunch at a restaurant on Lido Isle when a woman came up to us and admired Derek in his mother's arms. She looked at me and said, "Your son will bring you great honor someday."

Childhood

Derek grew up surrounded by family and grandparents. He was athletic, well-spoken, and loved by everyone. After completing grammar school, Derek wanted to play Little League baseball, so when he was eleven years old I decided to coach his team. After all, I had experience as a professional ballplayer and UCLA baseball coach.

I had started my third and most successful company two years prior, and it allowed me the time to coach and travel with the team. Based on my experience in baseball I was able to teach the boys the fundamentals of how to throw and field the ball by position, run the bases, work the count, hit and run, and understand the game. We developed the most important ingredient to any team: team chemistry. At the end of each practice I would have the boys run ten sixty-yard sprints for their conditioning and stamina training. After the second practice of doing wind sprints, the boys were exhausted and ready to drop. Derek approached me and said, "Dad, I don't like doing these wind sprints," and walked away in disgust.

I called Derek back in front of the team for what was to be a dramatic moment and said, "I am not your dad, and you call me 'Coach' at all practices and games, and when we are at home I am your dad." It was a defining moment for me to tell my son not to call me "Dad" when I was the coach. But it wasn't about me; it was how I had to gain the respect of fifteen boys who wanted to be part of the team's chemistry. Although Derek was my son, he was just one of many players on the team, and I wasn't going to show favoritism. He was going to be treated the same as all the other young players on the team. The team liked that exchange, and it was the basis for becoming a team. It was clear that Derek was not going to get any special treatment.

We had a good season that year and won the La Habra Little League division. From the eight teams the coaches picked fifteen players who would play for the La Habra Little League All-Stars. These players would play for the city, regional, and state championships, and the winner would go to the Little League World Series. Derek was a unanimous pick for the La Habra all-star team.

Derek pitched against and defeated the East La Habra All-Stars at Yorba Linda Stadium. The following game was the sectional championship for which our team qualified. As I made the starting lineup, I moved Derek down in the batting order. He came to me upset. Crying in the dugout he said, "How can you do this to me?"

I then benched him and removed him from the lineup. When his mother came over to me and wanted to know why her son wasn't playing, she asked, "How could you do this to our son?"

"It is a matter of team discipline," I said. "Now sit down and root for the team."

Derek's mother adored her son. She was very protective of him and was always the one to give in to his demands. Without honesty, love, and creating boundaries of discipline, children become entitled. And that was what led Derek into the behavioral tendency of: "If Dad says no, go to Mom, for that is the beginning of yes."

We got behind early in the game, and I summoned "Nalbandian" to warm up, as he was going to start the third inning. He pitched five scoreless innings and we came from behind to win regionals. I think over the years Derek remembered that experience and learned a certain humility and respect for others. We came to win through his dominant pitching but lost in the state championship. Overall a life lesson was learned: Be strong in all that you do so that you may succeed. Derek was well on his way as a student and athlete who had visions of going to the alma mater of his dad and two brothers: UCLA.

Uncle Archie

From the age of eighty-two until he was ninety, I took care of Uncle Archie and managed his estate. That was when Derek met Uncle Archie. He went with me every day to visit him at an assisted living home in La Habra, one mile from my home.

Derek loved Uncle Archie. Archie taught him how to play pool and talked to him about his life experiences as a ballplayer and businessman, and about the loss of his horse, Driftin' Along. Spending time with Uncle Archie, Derek was able to experience the capabilities of a self-made man with no formal education, who experienced life in the raw growing up without a mother, and with a father who was unable to speak English and therefore couldn't work. Uncle Archie always had the ingenuity to make things happen and created his success through hard work and persistence.

Derek spent nine years with this humble man. They developed a seemingly limitless soul connection and compassion. When Derek was twelve years old Uncle Archie passed away. His passing left Derek seeking answers as to why he had to leave us. Derek learned that death is final, but even though our bodies die, our spirits are alive and remain until the day when the Lord calls us home to live in eternity.

After Archie's death, Derek and I made a truth pact called "pinky swear" in remembrance of our mutual bond and respect for Uncle Archie. It meant that there would always be truth among us and that we would never lie to one another. It was our sacred bond and commitment of trust in honor of Uncle Archie's memory.

Derek was like every other kid growing up—loving, charismatic, demanding of self, and he exaggerated to get his way. However, he would never lie when I asked him to pinky swear. He would never break our truth alliance, and that was the ultimate truth.

Derek desperately strived to be the best in his competitive pursuits. It seemed that he wanted to be accepted, but he did not allow self-acceptance until he knew he achieved his goals. Peer pressure was a silent force that kept him from healthy relationships. He always used surfing as his outlet. He would liken himself to Uncle Archie—a gambler in surfing—always striving to be the best. Derek's intuition was always at work; we spent countless hours talking about business, and he would have insights and perspectives that were far beyond his years.

Phil

When Derek entered Corona del Mar High School, he was prepared to play baseball and continue his B+ average in his studies.

One day after school Derek came home and told my wife and me that the mother of one of his classmates was getting a divorce, had to move out of her apartment, and was going to live with another man. Derek said his friend, Phil, had no place to live and asked if he could come live with us.

Our lives were about to change. As I knew nothing about this young man, I told my wife I was going to do some research so we knew what we were doing. I did a background check and talked to our pastor. I learned there were many agencies that assisted families with these kinds of issues. Our church also had an outreach program for children separated from their parents, and I was eager to see what I could do to get Phil the help he needed to get back on his feet. In the end, Phil ended up living with us for about a year and a half. Our daughter, Jeanne, who was then a junior at Corona del Mar, was at home with us too.

Phil was bright, polite, clean, and neat. Derek became very close to Phil, who was persuasive and smart. The two of them became inseparable. Corona del Mar had seven hundred students, mostly from affluent families living in Newport Beach and Corona del Mar (Corona del Mar is known to have the highest income per family in the United States, and Newport Beach is ranked in the top ten). The academic standards there are very high, and the curriculum is set to prepare the students for leading universities such as Stanford, UCLA, Harvard, and Princeton.

I first became suspicious of Phil when money went missing from my wallet. My wife declared that I must have misplaced my money. On Sundays we would go to church as a family, but Phil declined to attend. It was the beginning of what I called the "Rasputin" effect upon our family. Rasputin was the evil man who gained favor with the wife of Russian Czar Nicholas, Alexandra, who trusted him to bring healing to her hemophilic son, Nicholas II. Alexandra's perception of Rasputin as a healer later turned fatal. Phil had that effect on us; I came to realize he could do as he pleased and nobody would doubt or question his actions because of their pity for him for being "homeless." Derek and his mother were his most prominent targets.

Derek was greatly influenced and became dependent on Phil. He also possessed a power over my wife who was hypnotized with sympathy and didn't want him to be out in the cold world. It was then that I realized that the relationship between my wife and me was no longer built on trust and respect and love. After seventeen years of marriage, I realized it would never be the same. Incredibly, this played out over the next ten years of our life together, but this realization would ultimately lead to the dissolution of our marriage and final divorce. Another takeaway.

Soon after my suspicions about Phil began to materialize, I learned that he was part of a drug distribution ring at school. At one parent-teacher conference, several parents confronted me and asked if I was aware of the drug dealing. I told my wife about this and she denied that Phil would be part of such a thing. She went on to tell me that Phil had helped Derek immensely in his studies and that his grades could be attributed to Phil's influence.

In his sophomore year, Derek quit playing baseball and took up surfing, just like Phil, a pothead surfer (though I didn't know that at the time). Phil had about ten surfer friends that were in his program. Derek got really good at surfing and received several sponsorships—Volcom, Stussy, Quicksilver, and others later. He became quite a well-known surfer in Southern California and even surfed San Onofre, Lower Trestles, Surf City, Pipeline, and later, the Wedge.

I came to learn that the surfers thrived on marijuana to relax and uppers in order to be creative and somewhat fearless. Derek had started using marijuana, progressed to uppers, and began experimenting with habit-forming drugs without my knowledge. Derek also became a top skateboarder in a marijuana and uppers-laden environment where young people smoke and use to stay relaxed and stay on top of their game. The social kids, I learned, liked drinking beer or alcohol with marijuana in preparation for college. The "Rasputin" effect was in full swing and I was powerless to stop it.

At that point we lived in the exclusive community of Cameo Shores in Corona del Mar, and I owned my successful patented growing system business. I had just landed the Home Depot account with their 250 stores in Arizona and Southern and Northern California. It was a major undertaking and I was involved in setting up the strategies and distribution to their network of stores. You can really get caught up in the undercurrent of life, and there is no getting off.

The only time I saw Derek during this time was in the evenings and on the weekends when he was not surfing. While

I had raised Michelle, Steve, and Jon and was able to instill in them important family values and provide a framework for their success, I was now consumed with my growing business. It demanded my full attention.

Derek wanted to surf the famous Wedge, so I surprised him by moving our family to an oceanfront home a block from the Wedge on Balboa Peninsula. Surfers from all over the world came to surf the Wedge, and Derek fit right in with the best of them. Since I had learned that Derek was getting all of his drugs from Phil, I told Phil we were moving and he would have to leave. However, the Rasputins of the world never really leave; they linger, always attached to their subjects. It is a form of addiction. Phil moved on when we moved, but in a way he never left.

Troubled Times

When Derek was seventeen years old and a junior in high school, I began to notice behavioral and dietary changes. I asked him if he was still taking prescription medications for some surfing injuries he'd had. Derek responded with a convincing, "No, Dad."

In his last semester at Corona del Mar, Derek was one of thirteen students expelled for a prank that the boys played on the school principal. And it was worse than just boys being mischievous; there were drugs involved. One of the boys from a prominent Newport Beach family was getting recreational drugs and joints from his family and selling them to the other boys, which seemed to be common throughout the community. Derek was one of the top surfers in Orange County and on the prestigious CDM surf team, from which he was promptly dismissed. He would also have to go to a GED school to complete his high school diploma and could not attend the CDM graduation, which was highly esteemed by the students, the city, and was viewed as the gateway to a prolific future.

Derek was devastated that he would be unable to attend his graduation ceremony at CDM. Several of his friends were going on to UCLA, Stanford, and UC Berkeley. There were graduation parties and celebrations to which he was not invited, and that left him in a state of depression.

He came to me and he asked me, "Dad, why didn't you help me out so I could graduate with my class?"

"The principal and school administrators told me you destroyed school property and broke into the principal's office and damaged it."

"Dad, I went along with my friends. I didn't do anything. I just watched my friends get even."

"Derek, are you telling me you went along with this prank to be accepted or that you wanted to tag along?"

"Dad, I didn't do anything. I just watched them do it."

"Derek, there is accountability for being a part of a destructive and violent act."

I wrestled with Derek's logic and lack of responsibility. He knew better. It became apparent to me that something was missing in our relationship as father and son. It was then that I began to realize the power of peer pressure, that as a parent's influence diminishes, the child's worth becomes centered on acceptance from his peers. Derek was raised, I thought, with Christian values and great role models, having been raised with siblings who were A students in high school and had graduated from UCLA. I now needed to focus on how I could be a better dad to him.

As I am writing this story, I have learned of thirty OD's (overdoses) in the last two weeks in the Newport Beach area, not including teen suicides from bullying and peer pressure. I have learned that several local boys have died as a result of overdosing. I thought these kids were "real" addicts while—although involved in drugs recreationally—Derek's use was medicinal for his injuries and chronic ear pain related to surfing.

I took him two weeks later to be drug tested, and he tested positive. To his mother's dismay I grounded him until he got clean. A personal note here: All kids know how to pass any and all drug tests with urine samples. The only way to learn if your child is free of drugs is by testing the hair follicles on their head.

Taking a step back for a moment, I came to realize that Derek and his peers were looking for acceptance. Acceptance was elusive and it would never satisfy or bring inner peace to their lives. The social climate in Newport Beach was eclectic and demanded you be "seen" at public gatherings, attend shows, and entertain at your beach homes.

Drugs alter your perceptions and your needs become dependent on what brings you pleasure. I really thought I was there for Derek. I accepted him as my son and was proud of his accomplishments, but I did not realize the role that drugs played in his life. I loved him unconditionally, but it was never enough. I gave Derek everything in the way of material things and taught him the Christian values I was raised with, but as my business grew and became more successful, the demand grew for more time away, as that is the way of life in building a business.

Competitive Surfing

At twenty-two years old, Derek was gaining "acceptance" for his surfing abilities and continued to smoke marijuana to stay on top of his game. There was something about marijuana that had a calming effect on him. At that point it was not an addiction per se, but we later learned that when marijuana is used with other drugs, the addiction begins to take hold. I was trying to understand the demands and pressure of competing. When I played professional sports, the players used chewing tobacco, drank booze, and smoked. I had tried chewing tobacco and got deathly ill when I was trying to get accepted as a rookie pitcher. I did not realize you were supposed to spit out the juice when chewing instead of swallowing it. Talk about trying to get accepted!

Peer pressure, recognition, acceptance. These are all ongoing battles for young adults, especially when parents are not on the same page as one another. I was caught up with a growing business that provided status, recognition, and acceptance. And living at the beach in Newport, you were labeled "rich" as well.

Derek's sponsors wanted him to surf competitively. He was winning all the local tournaments and they wanted him to enter the national surfing contests, but all the while he was taking his pain medications and marijuana to stay on top.

Derek continued to excel in surfing and strived for acceptance by winning contests. He became known as the "Fearless One" at the Wedge, as he would take the biggest waves and always play to the crowds. Each September the surf at the Wedge reached fifteen to twenty feet. All the local TV stations covered the surfers for a week with standing room-only crowds from all over Southern California. Derek always stood out and would stay around to sign autographs for the youngsters who were in awe of him.

Derek had always wanted to be invited to surf the fifty-foot waves at Waimea on the North Shore in Hawaii where you are tugged out by a boat to ride the colossal wave. It is only for the most experienced surfers. We met Ken Bradshaw, legendary for surfing Waimea and other big surfing areas throughout the world. Derek had just completed a contest and told Ken of his dream to surf Waimea. Ken took a liking to Derek and helped him train for the big surfing events where he was able to compete and earn money, like Pipeline, Bali, Australia, Costa Rica, Todos Santos, and Lower Trestles.

With all the pressure for his upcoming surfing events, Derek was practicing at the Wedge for an event in Australia. He was attempting to take a twenty-foot wave when he was thrown from his surfboard, thrown eight feet into the air, and had the terrifying experience of almost bleeding to death when the tip of his surfboard landed up his rectum.

I was notified at my office as Derek was being transported to the Hoag Hospital Trauma Center. When I met the doctor, he told me that he would have to do emergency surgery and that there were complications, that, in effect, Derek would no longer be able to have his bowel movements normally, that they were going to attach a sack that would have to be emptied after each movement.

I told the doctor that my son was only twenty-two years old and in no way would I want him to live that way. I called our family physician right away and explained what happened. He told me he would send a specialist over right away and instructed us to do nothing until he arrived. After thirty minutes Dr. Barak Rad, a colorectal specialist, arrived and examined Derek immediately. After an eternity he came out and told me that Derek had severed his sphincter muscle in his rectum. Luckily there was one centimeter of muscle, and immediate surgery could restore normal rectum and bowel use. Needless to say, Dr. Rad is rad, and he is my personal doctor for my colonoscopies every five years.

After the incident, Derek and I had a father-son, heart-to-heart conversation. "Derek," I started, "do you realize that you could have bled to death if you weren't seen by someone in the dusk hour? Do you realize someone called your mother who transported you to the hospital?"

"I know, Dad, but I was practicing a new maneuver that most surfers can't do."

"Don't you practice with your fellow surfers around?"

"They were surfing at another beach and practicing in a calmer surf."

"Why didn't you do the same thing and practice with them?"

"Dad, I made the team to go to Australia, and none of those guys made the team."

"Where are the surfers that made the team?"

"Some live in Hawaii, one in La Jolla, and one from Coco Beach, Florida."

"Do you realize that you are lucky to be alive?"

He looked at me. "Dad," Derek said, "I guess it wasn't my time."

Derek was back surfing four weeks later. The other surfers could not believe his comeback. You see, if you have faith, what is taken away prepares you to come back later. Derek's dramatic accident was a takeaway and an awakening that trying to be the best and being fearless was not the way to earn acceptance. First, it is necessary to respect and accept yourself for who you are. Realizing who you are and respecting yourself breeds inner confidence and self-acceptance. The comeback was Derek's eventual realization that drugs and surfing were not how he got acceptance.

Derek told me afterwards that he was quitting drugs and wanted to prepare himself to be one of the best surfers in the country. I knew through our family history that he could reach those heights. He was a gifted athlete after all.

Entrepreneurial Beginnings

After he got his GED, Derek came to me and told me he wanted to turn his life around but did not know how. I told him that going to college was a start in the right direction. He enrolled in Orange Coast College in Costa Mesa and began taking courses in horticulture. He was already adept at growing plants in my patented growing system and knew all of its inner workings.

He was doing very well on his college surf team when he incurred another serious injury to his neck and knee during competition. The doctors prescribed Valium and other pain-relieving medications, and that was the beginning that would take him down another path.

After Derek's surfing injury, he came to me and said he would like to become a grower of palm trees and ornamental foliage using my patented subirrigation system. Derek had a very inquisitive mind and wanted to learn firsthand how our grower group was growing large volumes of foliage that prevented overwatering and kept plants healthy and vibrant.

While I was president and CEO of my company, I started Derek growing the most exotic palms, the Rhapis and Kentia palms, which are the most in-demand and expensive for the commercial markets. He learned to grow in a small greenhouse since it would take the palms a year to a year and a half to grow seven to nine feet, and he would be able to sell them at forty dollars a foot. He loved growing and began growing all varieties of herbs and tomatoes, which led him to growing fruit trees. He had a nice clientele, and at the same time he was learning the ropes to running a business. Derek had adopted my entrepreneurial creed by Napoleon Hill: "Whatever the mind can conceive and believe, it can achieve." Derek was becoming more knowledgeable, developing the skills needed to build a foundation that would support him in the coming days.

Derek called me and was excited to let me know he was starting his own business. It would be called Botanical Brothers, an e-commerce company where he could sell not only the growing system, but also the foliage and fruit trees grown in the system.

Everything seemed to be going well. Derek was doing trade shows to broaden his base. Later I learned he had become a big Bob Marley fan, an icon in the cannabis world for his reggae music. His legacy carried on after his death at a young thirty-six years old. I learned later that Derek had made inroads with the hippies and those in the pot-smoking culture; he continued smoking marijuana to supplement his pain medications. Derek was now twenty-six years old, living his own life and earning seven thousand dollars a month.

Derek began traveling the world and made connections in Amsterdam, eastern and western Canada, France, and New York (with the *High Times* editor and international cannabis guru

Danny Danko). People from all walks of life loved his passion, energy, and creativity, and he was always looking for ways to help people in need. The bond Derek shared with Uncle Archie and me was his motivation and driving force to succeed.

Derek continued to suffer chronic pain from his surfing and skateboard injuries. His ear pain had become an infection, and he was given OxyContin to relieve his pain on an as-needed basis.

In spite of his skill in growing ornamental foliage and herbs, his passion was to grow cannabis as a medicine for people dealing with severe pain from cancer, arthritis, joint damage, chronic disease, anxiety, muscular pain, coping, and migraine headaches. He hoped to help provide relief and wellness; in essence, he wanted to stabilize the immune system and bring people back to health. It was a major undertaking for a young man of twenty-six with no formal college education, but he knew that his only limitation was his imagination.

Through his network Derek came into contact with many people who believed in his growing techniques. He traveled the country with Danny Danko, who was intrigued with Derek's ideas and the results he was getting in our growing system. He was one of the most respected innovators and cultivators in the cannabis industry, and he took Derek on a tour to meet major growers throughout Canada, Colorado, New York, and the Triangle in Humboldt County. Most growers were old-school and grew more for the pothead culture, but Derek's new ideas intrigued them. He began developing relationships with the old culture and worked with growers to cultivate "clean" cannabis to be used for medicinal purposes. In turn, this would change the perception of cannabis being an addictive drug. Many growers took to his new approach to make cannabis a healing medication, the need for which stemmed from Derek's own experience of suffering from acute injuries and knowing that prescription drugs lead so many to addiction. Derek was in constant conflict with his Christian upbringing. In spite of his drug use, he felt his real purpose was to help others and be a reflection of the teachings of our Lord.

In the process, Derek earned lots of money. He was climbing the ladder with his unrelenting passion to grow everything for the betterment of the environment. He was always striving for an elevated self-esteem. The underlying need to prove himself haunted him, even from that young, tender age of twenty-six. He had a nice house near the beach, a new car, and everything a twenty-six-year-old would want (even without a college education).

Through his acquaintances I later learned that Derek had met a lot of people who became envious of his success and what he was trying to promote. Still, there was always the need to show how successful he was. He adopted the label "promoter," but not for his desire to bring a new methodology that would change the perception of marijuana as a healing herb.

As a father I was proud of my entrepreneurial son and believed he was building something special, but I did not see or comprehend the path he had chosen in terms of drugs. How does such a young man manage to diverge from a loving family with two older brothers, two older sisters, having grown up in a Christian home?

When people feel insignificant and unsure of their status in life, they look to false standards to make themselves important. They speak in superficial, temporary, and unimportant terms. In retrospect I saw Derek but comprehended what I wanted to see. You see, Derek never had the managerial skills and experience to run a business, but he always had rolls of cash. He perceived this as success, albeit an addictive success.

A Difficult Path

Derek met and got involved with some buddies who liked to gamble. He was drawn in by his need to be important, successful, and accepted, which caused him to take a path that proved to be fatal six years later.

Derek moved in with a friend named Zach who was a good student and an up-and-coming musician. He was a bright kid studying finance whose father was a prominent CPA in Orange County. Together they rented a nice home in Dana Point, another good surfing area. Zach had formed a band and did weekend gigs at popular restaurants throughout Orange County.

Derek relayed to me that his accountant said his business was making money. I later learned his accountant was his roommate, Zach. He had no idea what a financial statement was, let alone a balance sheet.

Derek would always call me and tell me what his next move was. One day he decided he wanted to bring in a business partner to further his growing business. Derek only listened to what he wanted to hear, and that is where his education failed him. As president and CEO of my company, I was earning $250,000 annually. One day Derek came to visit me with a business opportunity and proceeded in all seriousness to ask me to become his business partner, that I could double my salary in one year if we worked together.

Was it brilliance or ignorance that lay deep within as Derek believed he was changing the world so that people wouldn't have to suffer any longer by taking prescription medications? Derek was persistent and told me of the global harvest in growing medical cannabis, that he had lined up a grower network in Amsterdam, Canada, and the U.S.

Derek believed in everything he did and had an ad agency working for him full-time that truly believed in him. They built websites, ran ad campaigns, printed brochures, and marketed his products. Derek gave the owner of the agency 25% of his company. The agency seemed to help his business grow and had set up a new banking system for him. However, a conflict arose with the agency; Derek learned they were siphoning money from his account. What looked like a promising venture became another takeaway—another setback—that would change his course of business and his way of thinking.

Derek had learned that a circle of his friends had their own scheming business pursuits. All were taking uppers and anything else that gave them highs and kept their energy up. I later learned they had a distribution group of over fifty people who were getting pain-relieving drugs from another group and selling them on the street for profit.

Once again I saw things in Derek's life that I thought were good and that overall Derek was doing well. I was still heavily involved in the daily demands of my growing business and did not see that Derek's lack of experience in building and running a business was only driven by his passion to succeed at all costs. In hindsight I missed the big picture. I saw only what was tangible to me and not the fabric that the illusion was woven into.

Ryan

I knew Ryan growing up in his teens, a surfing buddy of Derek's. He was handsome, charismatic, and always proper and respectful in my presence. His dad was a developer and built luxurious oceanfront homes in and throughout Newport Beach. His dad was very successful, but when he learned of his wife's numerous affairs he divorced her. Ryan became desolate. His mother got one of the oceanfront homes as part of the settlement. She became an alcoholic and married a man she could control with her self-acclaimed affluence. Ryan's dad later met a Chilean woman and moved to Chile. Ryan was left alone to succumb to peer pressure and the surfer culture where marijuana was prevalent. I was unable to decipher the drugs that he and Derek were taking as the boys always remained cool and under control in my presence.

Ryan's lack of a solid family foundation negatively affected him. He experimented with other drugs like OxyContin and cut heroin, and he eventually needed the drugs in order to function. He left the surfing world but would always call or stay in touch with Derek. One day Derek returned home from surfing practice and went by Ryan's opulent apartment by the beach that his dad gave him. He found Ryan barely breathing. Derek called me and told me Ryan was barely conscious, that he was suffering from an old affliction and needed care. Derek seemed to know the symptoms. He fed and bathed Ryan daily with my help as a surrogate father.

About a month later, Ryan was feeling better and was acting like himself. It was then that I realized he had been detoxing, ridding himself of the drugs in his system. His dad came for a visit and told me of his new life in Chile and thanked me for being a dad to Ryan. He left shortly thereafter, returning to his new life, leaving Ryan on his own once again. Derek became a "bro" to Ryan and worked to get him a job and begin life anew.

Later, Ryan would be one of the two hundred surfing "bros" that paddled out to sea to sprinkle Derek's ashes.

Divorce

Derek was twenty years old when a heartbreaking takeaway came, and it was part of the most devastating time in my life as well. On my sixty-fifth birthday, two of my children told me that my wife of twenty-seven years had been having a yearlong, inappropriate relationship with my daughter's boss, a man who was not only ten years younger than my wife, but whose current wife was pregnant with their first child.

It was a tumultuous time for the whole family. The woman I had trusted for twenty-seven years in raising my children and stepchildren had broken our family and felt no remorse. She began a relentless attack on my three children, blaming them for the breakup. Four months later, during our divorce, she was invited to stay with a gentleman business client in England and decided to move in with him and his children. She married him two and a half years later.

Derek and his sister were disillusioned and hurt beyond words, especially after the abrupt departure of their mother leaving for a new life. Derek was torn. He loved his mother but was deeply conflicted about her dishonesty and failure to ask for forgiveness. He became confused and troubled, which led him further into despair. It was unbearable for him to lose the love of his mother. I witnessed Derek's decline—the rejection, the pain from lack of acceptance. It was all-encompassing and began taking a toll on his mental health and negatively affected his business.

The scar on Derek's heart was permanent. He couldn't handle her deception, how she had used him to keep her ongoing relationship secret. I believe that Derek's pain and the loss of his mother catalyzed his renewed need for drugs. When there is separation in love, there is a void—a hole in the heart. A broken heart is a condition that depletes all your strength, energy, and drive, and challenges your belief system and relationship with our Lord.

I was devastated, brokenhearted, and disillusioned, and was dealing with feelings of fear and inadequacy in the aftermath of my divorce. You feel like you are in a bottomless pit with no way out. A darkness comes over you and you don't know what to do next. Through it all, though, devastation leads to hope, and losing can become winning. The takeaway became the new path to a big breakthrough in my life.

My life changed from a state of devastation to one of hope in a period of one year. Derek came to me, and his spirit was comforting and loving. Through his caring I began to find the love that I knew my children had for me, and I felt I could reflect and begin to find my way back.

Derek eventually told me that his mother asked him to keep her relationship secret. This proved damaging. Derek had been taught trust and respect, but someone he was supposed to trust and respect most had betrayed him. That trust was broken. Self-preservation became his method of survival.

After living on the Balboa Peninsula for eleven years, I decided to move to Laguna Beach and had Derek come live with me. He was great. He was really there for me, cooking and making sure I was okay until I got a grip. He would always console me by reminding me that God doesn't make mistakes, that He would take care of me. Such a loving quality from a young man who was dealing with his own hurt.

I finally got a divorce settlement by giving my wife a home and all my material assets. I was able to hold on to my business, which was now struggling, but a peace came over me. Derek and I became close as father and son.

Derek moved out on his own. He was still involved in his business and trying to understand why his mother had left. In his desperation Derek made a deal with his mother to distribute throughout Europe and Canada where he had connections. However, that idea failed miserably. Derek went to his mother in England; I had given her the U.K. patent rights to manufacture our old subirrigation growing system. She had built the tooling and was distributing in England. Derek went to bring her system to California for distribution. When my board of directors learned of this, they rejected Derek's proposal to distribute under my patent agreement with his mother.

The divorce, the rejection, and the guilt were too much for Derek to overcome. Failure subsumed his life. He tried to regain his aura, his passion, by going back to community college to find his purpose in cultivating plants again in conjunction with a horticulture professor. The school was considering him for a position as greenhouse grower, which would involve growing fruits, vegetables, and herbs to sell to faculty, students, and their families. The scope of work expanded to growing poinsettias for the Christmas season. Derek knew how to grow poinsettias well; he had learned from the Paul Ecke Company in Encinitas, California—one of my customers and the largest grower of poinsettias in the U.S.

Derek came to me on cloud nine about this new start, this new opportunity to rekindle his status and prominence as a grower. He would be able to generate revenue for the school and for himself. He sold the school on growing in our patented growing system. After sixty days the school's budget committee turned down the viable program that the professor and Derek had developed. Rejection. Another takeaway. His spirit was crushed and doubt crept back in.

Morgan

A few months later there was a new development. It was as though the Lord was watching over Derek.

Some people live a long time searching for the meaning of life but never obtain the spirit and power that Derek was about to receive. The power was an attraction of spirit, which always gave him a presence. When one door closes, another door opens.

Derek met a beautiful young lady, a hair stylist and partner in a well-known company based in Manhattan named OuiDad. Morgan was attractive and charismatic and full of life. She owned a salon on eclectic Montana Street in Santa Monica and had a who's who of clientele. She was financially successful at the age of twenty-seven.

Derek and she were soul mates from the beginning, and there was a spark in Derek that I had not seen for a while. He would call and tell me about this woman who had opened his heart and mind with hope and love. It was the perfect stimulus to propel Derek's life forward.

After they began dating, Derek left his rented house and moved into Morgan's home in the coastal town of Redondo Beach. She was instrumental in helping him start a new business through a generous investment based on a belief in their future life together. They were both twenty-seven years old when they began their life journey together. Derek started his business in Santa Monica and appeared to be doing well. One day he called with an excitement that a father loves to hear from a child. "Dad, I am going to be a dad!" It was a time of joy, and I felt joyous and ecstatic at the thought of being a grandparent.

Morgan continued to support Derek in every way until Derek called me and said he needed a loan. He told me he had used up the $25,000 that Morgan had given him, that he had had some bad luck and needed $10,000 to help sustain his business. He did not reveal how the money had been utilized, and he did not tell Morgan he was out of money. Hiding behind the truth was unfortunately a familiar way of life that Derek had revisited. Those that did not understand were often hurt by this deception.

Derek came to my home to discuss the matter, and it was a wake-up call for me. He rambled through his presentation and told me that he would quadruple my investment of $10,000. My business acumen came into play. I could see his plan was skewed and desperate and lacked the mechanism of an ROI (return on investment), which is essential to any proper investment.

I saw his eyes glaze over in disappointment. I had never turned him down financially to aid him in his pursuits. I believed he was gifted, and he had made a lot of money before, but this time I told him I could not invest because his proposal did not include a repayment plan for Morgan. I learned in that moment that what is wrong cannot be made right, and that what is missing cannot be recovered (Ecclesiastes 1:15).

Dad Life

The baby came nine months later. A beautiful bouncing boy named Velzy, named after the legendary Hawaiian surfer and board shaper, Dale Velzy, Derek's idol. Derek would always surf the North Shore on a beach named after him. It is still there today, and Morgan has taken Velzy there several times to learn how to surf and to understand his father's love for the sport.

Morgan was in love with Derek and knew of his need for prescription drugs. Derek's doctor had changed his medication from Valium to OxyContin. Due to his residual chronic pain from his surfing days, which had settled in his neck, back, knees, and most recently his ears, he would often find himself screaming with no relief. As time went on he needed other pain medications that were unfortunately habit-forming.

Morgan was familiar with the symptoms of drug use; her older brother had overdosed at age twenty-seven. She seemed to manage Derek's errant and unpredictable behavior. Derek loved his son. He worshipped Velzy and promised on pinky swear that he was going to be a good dad to him. I was excited and thought my prayers were being answered.

When Velzy was two years old, Derek started teaching him how to surf. He would care for Velzy every day while Morgan was working four days a week.

Part VI

Getting Drugs | Getting Clean

The Ranch

Derek tried to get a job. On one occasion he was let go after a week. He had always worked for himself and had been his own boss. His need for prescription drugs altered his thinking and he became belligerent toward his supervisor and other workers. He was fired after two days on the job. Morgan was now supporting Derek and their son with the hope that Derek would find himself.

Little did I know that Derek was getting prescription drugs from two different doctors who prescribed OxyContin, Valium, and Fentanyl simultaneously with unlimited refills. This allowed Derek to purchase unlimited quantities at wholesale and sell them at retail for a profit. It was so easy and there was no one to scrutinize this illegal activity.

While I was on a cruise, my son Jon called me at 3:00 a.m. with an emergency. He said that Morgan had called and said that Derek was incoherent and needed to be checked into a detox facility as soon as possible. She had found the finest detox facility in the country called The Ranch located in Nashville, Tennessee. They had eighteen beds and only took the most advanced cases. The cost for one month was $40,000. Fortunately Morgan's insurance paid for 80%, and I wired Jon the balance. The next morning Jon flew a reluctant Derek to Nashville and he was checked into The Ranch to begin his detoxification treatment.

Derek was a model patient his first week at The Ranch. The Ranch is recognized and noted for its discipline for understanding the patient's affliction, its causes, and how to change. During his free time Derek would discuss with the seventeen patients a business opportunity with his company. I learned that he would boast how much money each one could make and that everything was seamless. The other boys were taken by Derek and all wanted to be a part of his business.

The following week Jon called me and said the counselor from The Ranch had called. Derek had broken into their pharmacy, took all the OxyContin, and distributed it to the patients. He told Jon to come back to Nashville and pick up Derek; he was being expelled immediately for his stealing and abhorrent behavior.

Crushing. Heartbreaking. Disillusioned. No words can describe the feeling when your child cheats the system that was ready to prepare him for a new life. At that point his need for satisfaction—what drugs gave him—outweighed his desire for accountability and a way out. There is something about addicts. They can disguise themselves. They can fabricate and manipulate you into believing what they want. It is their way to get their needs satisfied at all costs.

This was way beyond the tough love discipline. What you learn is that there is no amount of money you can give them to change or get help unless they make the choice to do so, and that is not easy to accept.

When Derek returned home, he was reunited with Morgan. Their relationship grew strained. Derek was now on a daily dose of drugs in order to "cope" and maintain a certain level of energy and to function in his daily activities.

I came to the painful realization that Derek lacked discipline. The discipline I thought I had instilled in Derek was overshadowed by the secret life he was living. A dichotomy forms when two parents are not consistent in raising their kids, which causes separation. As a result, Derek played each parent to meet his needs. I thought he had learned discipline when I coached Little League, sponsored him in surfing events, attended his surfing events, supported him in general, and was just there for him. I was his father, provider, facilitator, and friend, but did I really know him?

Peer pressure had been constant for Derek, and his friends in Newport Beach—to my surprise—were recreationally using drugs they obtained from their parents. I trusted my children to be honest, and in turn they had exhibited the discipline I taught them as a single parent. What happened with Derek was "pluralistic ignorance" on the part of his mother and me. We were two parents who were ignorant of the other's philosophies and methods of raising children, both unable to trust and respect each other. This leads to chaos and allows children to be unduly influenced by their peers where they find acceptance. Parents must take note of this inner conflict that allows our children to take the path of least resistance.

Hoag Hospital

Derek called me when I returned from my cruise, and I was cautiously optimistic to see the son that I had raised and loved. He told me he wanted to get clean and once again be a dad to Velzy. Morgan was for it. Derek told me that he was "born again," that he had found Jesus and that his sins were forgiven. He wanted to rid himself of the heavy burden he had been carrying.

Morgan continued to be supportive of Derek and was encouraged by his born-again experience. She felt that his newfound faith would open the way for Derek to be her partner and a dad to their son.

With the help of Derek's older sister, Jeanne, he agreed to check into Hoag Hospital for a thirty-day detoxification program. Hoag Hospital was widely respected and had a good track record for helping young people from fourteen to thirty-four years old turn their lives around.

After two weeks the patients were put into group therapy to create a space of interpersonal support where they could discuss their afflictions. All patients were in an advanced stage of drug use, but they were "curable." It was working well. The counselor told me that Derek was making real strides and was liked and respected by all his peers.

Family members were invited to visit each Sunday, and we were treated to delicious barbecue lunches with all the trimmings. We sat in groups with patients and their family members to observe their progress and witness the camaraderie of the group. My daughter and I observed a change in Derek, which gave us a reason for hope.

Each patient had a roommate, a toilet, a shower, a sofa, and a TV to view at selected times. Some of the patients, including Derek, went to early morning prayer meetings. Prayer and the support system from the therapy group were a big part of the detox program. About 35% of patients would make changes from these support systems alone, and maybe another 25% would still need to go through rehab.

We went to the completion ceremony for the thirty-day program. Those who completed the program successfully, including successful drug withdrawal, could move into a halfway house for rehabilitation to start a new life. Two counselors told me that Derek had completed the program with honors and that with his newfound faith, everyone was confident he was ready to move forward in his life journey. They did recommend attending AA three times a week to continue his rehab and maintain a support system. Again I was encouraged and optimistic.

Miramar

Derek went to a halfway house in Costa Mesa and was kicked out the second day for insubordination and lack of respect toward his counselor.

I was not notified, but Jeanne searched and found a local rehab center called Miramar. They were glad to take him in the next day based on recommendations from Hoag Hospital. Miramar was much stricter. No visitors were allowed during the thirty-day rehab process, and the patients had to abide by the stringent rules and regulations of the center. Upon completion of the program there was a graduation ceremony for the patients during which they received certificates denoting their successful completion of the intense therapy program.

Derek told me he was attending AA with a friend and really liked going since they talked about Christian love and support. He told me once again on our pinky swear, "Dad, I promise that I am going to be a dad to Velzy." Derek was finishing his third stint in rehab when his counselor called Jeanne and said that Derek would like his dad to pick him up.

The counselor said that Derek had detoxed and completed the intensive therapeutic rehab program that was required for him to graduate. He was now ready for rehab with a support system. My daughter, Jeanne, thought it best that Derek come and live with her, her husband Brian, and their daughter. Since she lived twenty minutes from AA, she decided that she could work and keep a close eye on Derek.

When I picked up Derek from his rehab center, we had lunch and talked over many things, including once again how ready he was to start his new life. He told me he had found what was missing in his life. I thought, *What a realization to come to!* I asked him to explain. He told me he had been hiding behind the pain from his injuries and had become dependent on medication to escape it. He went on to say that he was ready to start over since the drugs had taken over to the point that he could not think straight. I asked how he intended to start over. He told me by living with Jeanne and her husband, Brian. He would attend AA, and he had been promised a job with one of his golf pro buddies.

We arrived at Jeanne's condo. She had a beautiful bedroom downstairs for Derek, but he had access to the upstairs living and dining areas. Jeanne cooked all of his meals, did all his washing, and monitored his medications for chronic back and neck pain. We were all pleased with the process of his recovery, and he was excited to know that Morgan was bringing Velzy to spend the weekend with him.

Velzy was now two years old. He loved and adored his dad. All he knew was that his dad had been away on business and he was coming home soon. Being a grandparent, I had a heartfelt concern whether Derek—in his tenuous state—could establish a healthy and loving father-son relationship with Velzy. Our entire family was sensitive to this, and we were always there as a support system for both father and son.

Jeanne attended the AA meetings with Derek, and she was very encouraged about the relationships he was creating with the other members in this tried-and-true support group. Jeanne thought that after a couple of weeks he could attend by himself; the AA facility was only two miles from her home. Derek would always tell Jeanne how much he loved going to the meetings.

I thought things were going well. After a month Derek came

to me and said that he wanted to get an apartment of his own and had enough money for a down payment. Then he asked me for some money for living expenses. He said he had gotten a job at a prestigious golf club through one of his golf pro friends. He said he was going to caddy and earn three hundred dollars a day. Derek told me he loved his job, and I had a renewed faith that he was turning the corner, that he was beginning a path to a new life.

Derek went on to tell me that he was caddying for businessmen and making good tips. He told me he had gotten another job three days per week caddying at the five-star Pelican Hill Golf Course in Newport Beach. The golf course boasted vast views of the Pacific Ocean and was surrounded by homes worth upwards of ten million dollars. The cost to play the course was almost five hundred dollars for eighteen holes. Affluent people from all over the world came to play there. It was a special place to work and earn a good wage plus tips. Derek was assured of making around three hundred fifty to seven hundred fifty dollars a day or more depending on how many rounds he could serve in a day.

I wanted to play this prestigious course and thought I would go out to see Derek on the job. When I arrived, I asked where Derek Nalbandian was caddying today. The assistant pro replied, "Who?" I repeated Derek's name and he replied, "There is no one working at the club with that name."

Again, you come to a point where you think rehab has worked and your son is ready to move forward, but it was another disguise, another twisting of the truth. Rehab is only a step to clear your body of the drugs, but the ability to take control of your life is still suspect and, in Derek's case, this was missing altogether.

Ted

His name was Ted Caldwell, a university professor at the University of Southern California. I met Ted playing tennis on Saturdays at the Laguna Beach Tennis Center (which has some of the best players in Orange County). Tennis was a passion of mine. I had played on the Senior Tour and was ranked number three in doubles in the U.S. I played for the U.S. in 2000 and in the Australian ATP championship against ten countries. I was honored in the pre-tournament ceremony to carry the American flag before forty thousand people. David Nalbandian, who was a famous player from Argentina, is also a relative of mine. He was ranked number three in the world and is one of the tennis greats to have a winning record against the great Roger Federer.

One Saturday I was playing against Ted and won a very close doubles match. He came over to congratulate me and we struck up a conversation. We discussed our backgrounds and he asked me if I had any children. I told him about each of my five kids, and I expressed my deep concerns about Derek, that he had gone through detox twice and it hadn't worked.

Ted was seventy-three years old and told me he had been an addict for forty years—alcohol, marijuana, and other recreational drugs. He told me he lived with fear and depression and had no identity. His addiction was so bad that when he was teaching in his earlier years at another major university, he would drink a six-pack of beer to calm himself before giving a lecture, but he could never remember what he had conveyed to his students. Ted told me he was afraid of relationships growing up. Being an introvert, he would hide behind reading books and in that way he did not have to deal with his emotions. He said he liked girls but was afraid of rejection. He would wander off and take long walks to escape his feelings. He went on to college to get his degree and decided he would be most comfortable imparting the book knowledge he had accumulated over the years. He was able to succeed with the help of alcohol, marijuana, and uppers.

Ted asked me my ethnicity, and told him I was an Armenian-American. He told me one of his best students was of Armenian descent and had worked as the assistant deputy administrator for the Bureau of Humanitarian Response for eight years in the Clinton administration. Funny enough, his friend happened to be a very close friend of mine and was the president and CEO of a major Los Angeles corporation. When I called this close friend, Michael Mahdesian, to discuss my meeting with Ted, he said Ted was the best professor he ever had and they had studied together for a year in Geneva, Switzerland.

Ted and I had lunch a few times after that and he told me the startling facts of drug addiction. He described to me how addictions develop in stages. The first stage is experimentation—trying marijuana or uppers to feel pleasure, creativity, or some kind of empowering self-esteem. Ted noted that this stage brings awareness and pleasure-seeking thoughts, and the downside of use is lack of accountability.

The second stage is using drugs to bring immediate relief from anxiety, social inadequacy, and fear of failure and rejection from parents or friends. In this stage one's drug needs become stronger. The mind becomes charged with ideas and seeks pleasure, and when the drugs wear off the user experiences feelings of inadequacy and depression. In essence, the second stage is characterized by dependency.

The third stage is the most critical time for the addict. They have become dependent. If they become aware of their dependency they may want to make the choice to get clean. Ted spoke from experience and was emphatic that once the decision is made to get clean, there is no turning back. It is the choice of the individual. Remember, our children don't have a choice whether or not to be born. Derek was a product of a force he had no control over, and later on in life he chose to bring comfort and peace into his life through drugs. It wasn't the only path he could have chosen, but peer pressure and the pressure of acceptance was too much for him to overcome without a sufficiently strong foundation.

Ted told me that at Derek's current stage I should not give him any more money and that he needed a mentor and guide to help him through this critical and life-changing stage. He told me he would mentor Derek since he had worked with hundreds of young people. He had also worked with individuals whose choices were fatal. He had been there.

Ted told me he would take him to AA meetings three times a week and help him get a job through a priest friend of his that ran a rehab center in San Clemente, a group that works with those who want a fresh start and were willing to commit to the mentor's program. In turn they would get help, get cured, and return to society. It was all about choices.

I told Derek that Ted could be his mentor. Ted was going to help him overcome his addiction. Ted called and left Derek two voice messages. He called me when he did not hear back from Derek.

I called Derek and asked why he didn't call Ted back. He told me he called back and left a message on Ted's voice mail. I learned later that Derek had not called Ted back. It is at this stage, I learned, that one must see the truth of the addict and understand their disguise in order to understand their inability to be honest, which furthers their dependency.

Siblings

In addition to the rehab centers, Derek's siblings also provided an amazing amount of support, trying to help him get his life back on track. Derek grew up with his two brothers, Steve and Jon, and his older sister, Jeanne. Michelle was quite a bit older than he. However, each had a special role in Derek's life. He looked up to Steve who was an AAA airline pilot for American Airlines. He also looked up to Jon, with whom he surfed a lot. It was Jon who spent endless hours trying to help Derek through his drug use. Jon was also the one that called me when Derek needed to be checked into a detox center.

Derek greatly admired and trusted his oldest sister, Michelle, who was a software engineer for Cisco. Derek lived with her during his final days. Jeanne, Derek's other sister, was eighteen months older than he, and both were competitive in their sports endeavors. Jeanne was captain and an all-league water polo player at Corona del Mar, and Derek excelled in baseball and was number one on the high school surf team as a sophomore.

Confrontation

As parents we love our children unconditionally. We protect them with all our might, give them wings to fly to destinations of their choice, and we always pray for their safe return. I have always shared with my children a sage verse from the Book of John: "And ye shall know the truth, and the truth shall set you free."

When Derek fabricated the caddying job story to get me to believe that he was recovering from his addictions by working at prestigious golf clubs, it was a moment of truth. I reasoned that someone would recognize Derek's latent potential so he could work hard and take the necessary steps to get away from his compulsive need for drugs. "Wise words bring many benefits; hard work brings rewards" (Proverbs 12:14). Derek's brain was so diluted with the excessive pain medications that hoping and praying for a miracle was becoming hopeless.

I reasoned that Derek couldn't have consciously chosen this path. He was consumed by the power of the pain that he was suffering from his surfing injuries and skateboard accidents, and the only remedy he could choose from his doctors was the forbidding path of daily doses of OxyContin, Fentanyl, and later, heroin.

When I finally confronted him with his fabrication, he became angry and confrontational. His outburst was infused with desperation, guilt, denial, and virtual defeat. He told me he hated me, that I wasn't his dad. He was trying to diffuse his pain and guilt. I could see his eyes glaze over. Life was ebbing away from his soul and his recovery was in doubt. He was becoming a raging bull. I tried to reason with him but to no avail. It seemed as if he were transferring his pain to me so I could understand his grief, pain, guilt, and delusion. I told him over and over that he was my son and that I loved him. He told me to get away from him and that I was no longer his dad. My feelings went beyond understanding or hurt. I backed off and just cried until I felt relief from drowning in my tears of disbelief and the capacity to understand what it all meant.

I had to take a step back and give myself the space to come to terms with the reality that I was not prepared to meet. People had told me of the loss of their children as a result of drugs, car accidents, or drowning, and although you think of it, you never believe it can happen to you or your family. Another prophetic verse came to me later: "If you walk with me and follow my statutes and commands, I will give you a long life" (1 Kings 3:14). Our choices in life determine who we will become.

For thirty-two years Derek was my son, buddy, and confidant. That defining moment hit me so hard and with a force of pain that I will never forget. Today, as I remember that moment, I can only reason that Derek was robbed of his eternal spirit and had no control over himself.

Silence has a voice of its own. Silence is when you meet God face to face. We are not accustomed to this silence, for we are consumed with the business of life and the demands put upon us each day, but when you get there it is like a symphony and a great experience to discover.

Zionsville

The next day, my daughter Jeanne called me; they had organized a family meeting with Derek's mother. She had been unable to cope with his addiction and deal with the continued deterioration of his body and mind. Michelle was visiting from Zionsville, Indiana and offered to take Derek back with her to give him a fresh start away from his drug culture. Michelle was a single mom raising her teenage son, Cole, Derek's cousin. She had a beautiful five-bedroom home and lived in an exclusive community. She called me and said she felt the change of scenery could help Derek stay away from his network of friends who were tied to the drug scene.

Because Michelle was not knowledgeable about drugs, I discussed with her in detail Derek's three failed detox attempts, his habitual lying and wanting money, and his inability to hold a job and manage his personal affairs.

So, Derek flew home with Michelle, and during the first two days she said they felt each other out. She decided he could not use her car, but she would take him to AA three times a week and personally take him shopping for his personal needs. She would call me and say that Derek was doing well. They would talk about his childhood and his family, and he would finish by telling Michelle that he loved her and was happy to be living with her. Michelle felt there was hope for Derek and that change in his life was possible.

Part VII

Fire of Death I Illumination

The Final Act

There was a new home being built in Michelle's neighborhood, and she thought it might be a good idea if Derek went to speak with the construction superintendent about doing some work on the site. She was thrilled when he was hired as an assistant laborer to prepare, haul, and bring equipment to the workers' stations.

One afternoon Derek came home for lunch with Michelle. They had an engaging discussion about how he liked his job, was earning money, and that maybe he would buy a car. Michelle saw that Derek was alive and full of promise.

After lunch, Derek excused himself to take a short nap before going back to work at the construction site. After an hour, Michelle went into his room to awaken him so he could go back to work. She found him curled up and motionless as he lay on his side in bed. She tried waking him up, and to her horror she realized he was not breathing. She immediately called 911. The paramedics arrived and tried to resuscitate Derek, but to no avail. The paramedic noticed a syringe and concluded that it was an apparent overdose of OxyContin and heroin.

Michelle called me at about 6:00 p.m. and with trepidation told me Derek had died an hour ago. It was from an apparent overdose of drugs. She needed me to fly to Indianapolis immediately and would meet me at the airport. I made the last flight out that evening. On the flight I began to deal with rampant thoughts of depression, the loss of a son, a broken heart, and even anger. As a parent you are never ready to hear the words, "Your son is dead." Oh my God! Why? How did it happen? How could this happen? What did I do wrong? I was on a roller coaster headed to a state of oblivion.

It was a takeaway that every parent fears, the call that says, "Your child has had a serious accident," or in my case, "Your son died and you need to come identify and claim him." I tried to process the idea that Derek died; we always hope that there is still hope of recovery. But this was the final act. To say this was another takeaway is an incredible understatement. It is clearly one that may seem impossible to come back from, but nothing is impossible with God.

I arrived in Indianapolis at 1:00 a.m. Saturday morning. Once I arrived I did not have much time to think about Derek succumbing to his addiction; I needed to identify his body, pick up his remains, meet with the coroner, make preparations for what to do with his body, go to the mortuary, and comfort my daughter and grandson.

I found myself seeking answers when I arrived in Indianapolis. I tried to console Michelle since she had witnessed Derek's death and saw his warm, curled body lying on the bed. My grandson, Cole, who was seventeen years old, was in a state of shock. I was glad I was there to take over. You try to understand and reason things out, but nothing comes—only the same emotions that bring no comfort or reasoning power.

The next morning my spirit was awakened and I felt a calm come over me. The storm seemed to have subsided, and a peace came over me to the point that I was prepared to take care of what needed to be done. I was able to calm Michelle as she was overcome with guilt and felt responsible for Derek's death. Seeing Derek's motionless and unresponsive body was overwhelming for her and left an imprint that will remain with her for the rest of her life.

Having to take over the meeting with the coroner, making arrangements with the mortuary, and bringing Derek home for burial was God-sent and renewed my faith that God's presence is always there.

Memories

When I was raising Steve, Jon, and Derek, I thought about what beautiful memories we had made playing baseball, fishing, going to Angels baseball games, going to Disneyland, being a part of scouting trips, and going to church on Sundays. They loved our family vacations to Hawaii, San Francisco, and visiting their grandparents in Fresno. We had a large backyard with a full-size, half-basketball court with a regulation-size hoop and a forty-by-forty swimming pool to enjoy with all their friends and family. We were always having competitive half-court basketball games with our family and Jon and Steve's high school buddies.

My work ethic was central to my life, and in my younger years I had to compete to get what I wanted. As I started my family I taught the children the value of sports, the positives of winning and losing, sportsmanship, and the importance of competing to do your best whether you win or lose in the process. Being a good competitor brings you recognition, status, and acceptance. It teaches discipline and develops important skills for your life ahead.

Steve excelled in high school tennis and went to UCLA. He played varsity tennis against some of the top collegiate players in the country. Jon was a star baseball player in high school and received a scholarship to UCLA as a pitcher. He was later drafted by the Seattle Mariners. Jeanne played women's water polo in high school. She was an all-league and all-county all-star, and she played for Olympic coach John Vargas. She received a scholarship for water polo to the University of Southern California, but she chose Orange Coast College and finished second in the national championships. Derek competed in baseball and was on his way to becoming an excellent high school baseball pitcher when his peer group convinced him to take up surfing.

We always had friendly family competition. Every child was an A student in school. We also had a family spa. I remember spending hours with Derek after dinner discussing business ideas. He was very bright and had ideas that were ahead of his years.

I had wanted this relationship for Derek and his son—the ability to raise his son surrounded by family. I thought that being with family would help Derek and that we could be the support system he needed to turn his life around.

What Really Happened

Drug addiction is a chronic, often relapsing brain disease that causes compulsive drug seeking despite harmful consequences to the addicted individual and those around them. Although the decision to take drugs is voluntary for most people, the brain changes over time and challenges an addicted person's self-control and hampers their own ability to resist the intense impulse to take drugs. Derek's spirit gave out and was taken by his need to release the inner pain that he was never able to quiet.

I learned from Michelle that Derek was receiving daily overnight packages from his network of friends in a distribution network. Each shipment contained OxyContin. I was shocked that Derek had engaged with a group of young men who were all able to get prescription drugs from three doctors in Orange County. Each doctor, after writing the prescriptions, would receive significant sums of cash, which averaged out to be one dollar per pill and then sold on the street for between thirty-five and fifty dollars each. It was a cash cow, and it was run in conjunction with Derek's friends with whom he surfed over the years. Most of the young men came from affluent families from upscale beach communities.

I was just beginning to grasp the magnitude of what was transpiring when I was confronted with the decision of handling Derek's body and remains. The county coroner, Coroner Hough, called me and told me it was inadvisable to view Derek's body. He told me bluntly that I would not want to remember my son that way. He called again three days later with his findings, which I was able to comprehend and later cried tears to console my pain. Derek had consumed multiple drugs and basically overdosed by taking uncut heroin that he purchased from the construction workers.

Coroner Hough indicated that Derek had four Fentanyl patches all over his back and neck for pain relief. He said one patch was powerful enough to manage his pain and that his body was so medicated he was unable to exhibit any self-control; there was no clear state of mind when he took the uncut heroin and that he basically put himself into a deep sleep in order to prepare himself for eternity. The coroner went on to say he had never seen a case like Derek's with four Fentanyl patches. Either his pain was so acute or he was trying to release his emotional pain as well.

Fentanyl is an opiate used on patients after surgery and is one hundred times stronger than morphine. Deadly in small doses, Fentanyl is now being used by drug dealers and producers to spike doses of heroin for greater potency at a cheaper cost or as a counterfeit for another drug known as Norco. Fentanyl has been prescribed to cancer patients for decades, and is the most powerful painkiller available for medical treatment. It's typically administered as a lozenge, patch, or injection to patients with severe pain.

The coroner added that when Derek mixed the uncut heroin with OxyContin he was unaware of its potency; uncut heroin in Indiana was much stronger than in California where it was cut three to four times and was diluted. In California his actions may not have led to the overdose. He went on to say that Derek was so overmedicated he was powerless to think and prevent this from happening.

I decided that we would cremate Derek since his body was not suitable for viewing and so the memory of his spirit of who he was would smile upon us when he was ready to take his place in heaven. Then I would bring him back home for burial.

After five grueling days with the coroner, the mortuary, handling family concerns, and taking care of Michelle, I stepped away for a half day and walked down to a private lake punctuated with beautiful and colorful autumn leaves in the lovely town of Zionsville. It was so peaceful and I had time to reflect. I thought about how some people spend a lifetime studying the classics seeking enlightenment and the meaning of life but never obtain the spirit and power that Derek had. This essence of spirit was contagious and always gave Derek a presence. So why did he have to die? My early feeling was that Derek had disguised himself during his life; he had lost his God-given gifts of wisdom, understanding, love, faith, and sharing. Dependency and illusion took over. It was a very sobering moment of reflection, but it was only the beginning of what was to come.

What It All Meant

The day before I returned to Orange County, the mortuary called and said they had prepared Derek's ashes in three separate bags, cut his long hair for family members, and prepared the paperwork to carry his remains via a commercial flight without going through security. I packed his remains in my suitcase so I could carry them on the flight and have Derek with me at all times. It was a very surreal experience.

As I am a senior citizen, I have TSA identity clearance. I was preparing to go through the security checkpoint when a TSA security agent asked what I had in my suitcase. I told him it was my son's remains, and although he had no right (since I had the clearance documents prepared by the mortuary), he seized my suitcase as if I were a drug dealer. They proceeded to open my suitcase and wanted to open the box with Derek's ashes. I told him he was making a grave mistake and called for his supervisor. The supervisor questioned me and I handed him the certified papers. He immediately apologized for the audacious lack of respect. All I could think was, *Lord, forgive them, for they know not what they are doing.*

Pain has no limits and brings hurt that is unbearable. You ask, "Why do I deserve this?" But we soon learn that God uses pain in our lives to bring us to a better place. "Teach us to number our days that we get a heart of wisdom" (Psalms 90:12). Wisdom brings understanding. I have learned from Proverbs that if you lack wisdom, "get wisdom. Though it cost all you have, get understanding." This was the process that began to take place in my life.

Another biblical verse that was meaningful to me during this time of grieving was: "Give your heart to me that I may speak to your uncertainty, peace unto your worry, hope unto your disillusionment, and joy unto your sorrow." It was the power of truth from our creator who lifts us up, even from depths beyond our understanding.

Upon returning home, I made arrangements with Morgan to pick up Derek's ashes and locks of his hair. That day I received an outpouring of support and phone calls from Derek's friends—his "bros"—and acquaintances of his whom I didn't even know. We shared in our raw emotions and disbelief. We were all dealing with sympathy, sorrow, and the loss of a friend. Many shared that Derek's spirit would live on always and that he would be remembered for his surfing talents, especially for conquering the elite surfing areas. I was overcome by the love and compassion that the surfing community had for Derek. He was "accepted" and loved and would be remembered.

One of his close friends told me that Derek wanted to be like his dad, that Derek shared my values and faith in God and wanted to make me proud. He did love life and was always trying to help others. Derek would always take in those who were down and out, be it friends in need or stray cats. He would feed them, invite them into his home, and with his friends, he'd always encourage them that things were going to be okay. Listening to the countless stories from his friends and how he felt about his relationship with me hit me deeply and brought feelings of virtual helplessness, confusion, and despair from not being able to help him overcome his affliction.

I know the choices we make lead to our ultimate destiny. I am learning from this experience daily. It is a constant reminder about truth, trust, self-respect, and respect for others. I am still learning and growing from the loss of my son. It became apparent to me that our worst mistakes are the ones we do not notice. We don't take advantage of our incredibly hidden intuition.

I have gotten to really know Velzy. He is a beautiful, energetic young boy who has his dad's spirit and infectious smile. He tells me his dad comes to visit him at night and sleeps next to him. When I ask him how he knows, he tells me he feels his dad's bones next to him. Velzy says his dad lives in heaven and works there so he can help others. He helps God with people who like to surf. I always believed that our imagination is our only limitation, and what a gift it is to see Velzy exemplify that.

Morgan and Jeanne planned a wake for Derek the next day at one of Derek's favorite surfing spots in Laguna Beach. Over three hundred of Derek's friends attended, with one hundred of his surfing buddies who paddled out to sea to spread his ashes in his final resting place, the Pacific Ocean. There was a celebration of Derek's life that day, but it was accompanied by the sobering realization that his life was cut short and that Velzy had lost a dad.

After a month, Morgan called to come by with Velzy, and I was delighted. She brought Derek's handwritten diary to me and explained that Derek could not come to me and apologize for all the atrocities he had committed. He wrote meticulous notes from his heart that he could not verbalize aloud; instead the drugs controlled him and determined his ultimate fate.

Derek wrote some thoughts for me in particular that have given me a healing and peace going forward: "Dad, you have been my best friend, and I always wanted to be like you. I apologize for all the lies and hurt I caused you...Dad, I didn't mean to steal the money I took without you knowing because I intended to pay you back." In a cathartic articulation of his feelings, he could release his overwhelming guilt and the demons that had overtaken him.

Morgan went on to discuss Derek's last months with Velzy. His love was infectious but he was limited in his capacity to function normally. Morgan said she would have Derek sleep elsewhere since she did not want Velzy to see him during his periods of pain and depression. Derek's last days with Velzy were spent at the surf playing catch and going to a nearby arcade where Velzy got to play all the games.

Morgan tearfully explained Derek's struggles and what he tried to overcome, but his debilitating addiction was not forgiving. He told Morgan he was going to die soon and was preparing for the journey he knew he had to take. You ask yourself, *How can a person come to that choice, that decision?* But love is letting go. Derek's love for Velzy was the reason he had to let go. His final thought to Morgan was, "I love my son so much I don't want him to know who I am. I want to leave so he can treasure the memories we built together."

I listened to this account of a man suffering, of a man full of life who was charismatic, handsome, a world-class surfer, and had a son to share his life with that was his carbon copy. I thought, *How could anyone make a choice like that?* Trying to understand was painful, but pain teaches us how to overcome and understand.

When four months had passed, I began to see things in a positive way with my loving partner's help. She is my soul mate. My perceptions were not always clear, but colors were vibrant and I was alive in spirit. I worked out daily—walking, swimming, playing tennis—to ease the thoughts that were still fresh. If you allow the thoughts to persist, you stay hostage to fatigue, sorrow, and sleep. My daily walks connected me with who I am and gave me an appreciation for all the blessings I had in my life. Having a relationship with God brings wisdom and understanding to our spirit, which guides our journey in this life.

My partner and I share devotions each morning and our relationship is empowered by our love, trust, and respect for each other. We love to walk together on the beach and take in the beauty that surrounds us each day. We listen to the birds and to talk to people in and around our neighborhood to share our thoughts and love. We always share time with our dogs, Daisy and Poppy, who bring us great joy and love. Daisy is charismatic and is loved by everyone who meets her. She is a beautiful dog whose spirit speaks to you.

I was always there to forgive Derek, to try and help him with finances, rehab, groceries, car repairs, surfboards, and new cars, but that kind of forgiveness is shallow and does nothing to change the inner being of a person. Forgiveness is acceptance, love, and understanding a person's soul. Forgiveness does not judge. Forgiveness is God's healing ingredient for our inner soul, and the gift of healing is reconciliation, which has no limits.

I thought a lot about forgiveness regarding Derek's life. Jesus taught us about forgiveness. When the adulteress was going to be stoned to death for her sinful ways, Jesus said to the Jewish Sadducees, "He who is without sin, let him cast the first stone." The greatest example of forgiveness is when Jesus was nailed to the cross of Calvary and was spit upon and tortured because people could not accept His message of hope, righteous living, and living in selfish indignation. He cried out to our heavenly Father, "Forgive them, for they do not know what they do." I have forgiven Derek, for he was my son whom I loved dearly, and he brought a joy and happiness to my life that will forever stay with me.

Overcoming a child's death is not a place you eventually arrive at, but rather a path you walk. I am learning that each day we live. To gain perspective, I seek prayerful understanding so that I may grow from this unexpected experience. I believe that this is not a part of a parent losing a child; I prefer to believe that Derek was lent to me to raise for his time on Earth. In time, people need to know you have stabilized and moved on with your life so they can come back to you in confidence that it will not or could not happen to them.

Grief

There is a grief that overcomes you; it comes on like a rushing current. As I experienced firsthand, grief brings different levels of pain, stinging, and burning to your inner being, and unimaginable hurt. You cannot imagine the levels grief brings you to, especially when you are not prepared.

Grief is exhausting. It is like running away from a fear that has been deep within you and you cannot let go. Grief is sneaky. It has a way of creeping up on you when you least expect it and brings a heaviness that drags you down, down, down. Down is a bottomless pit that you fall into when you are overcome with grief and death. The pit is dark, damp, and is filled with the pity seekers that find no comfort and relief. Those people lack faith and take the ride down and never find their way out, for their choice is pity, sympathy, "poor me." We all have the power to get up, up, up and away to begin anew.

I have heard about grief symptoms from others: blurred vision, chest pains, heart palpitations, and an overwhelming fatigue that dulls you beyond being normal. One person told me of an out-of-body experience wherein they succumbed to the fear and remarkably came back. They said they went with their loved one and found them in a place where there was light leading them on a path where there appeared to be angels waiting for their loved one. They were able to let go and journey back.

Your mind drifts through each experience and you wonder how your loved one's life will turn out based on their choices. A friend shared with me during my grief that, "Children are a gift we receive on terms we aren't allowed to negotiate. Accepting those terms is our gift to them for however much time we are allowed to have together in our lives."

There is an inadequacy that comes over you and you feel helpless. God did not mean for one's child to die first, and all kinds of questions taunt you as you try to rid yourself of the guilt and anger to deal with the pain of loss. You ask God for comfort and yes, He was there to give me comfort that I could begin to understand. "As a Father has compassion on His children, so the Lord has compassion for those who love Him" (Psalm 103:13). I have known that love is understanding and conquers our fears, doubts, and brings hope and resolve to us. As it says in Proverbs, "Love of the Lord is the beginning of wisdom and knowledge of the Holy One is understanding."

When grief hits you, you look where to turn. I turned to the cross where Jesus died for each of us. His life was taken so that we may have life and understand that death is not a final act; it is the beginning of eternal life. God has promised us this as His children. Jesus was a child who was raised to bring God's omnipotent love to the world, a love that changes each life so

118

that life may have purpose and fulfillment, yet each day gives us challenges and fears, even the death of a child.

We all have our takeaways and have the choice to be bitter, upset, cheated, or envious, or we can accept our fate and deal with the setback. With the right attitude, you can choose to exude positive energy and allow your comebacks to come to you. We have a spirit with no limitations; it is how we make choices that determines our fate in life. As James Faust communicates in his sermon "The Refiner's Tale," having passed through the fire of death either melts you or illuminates you. The choice is ours to make.

Epilogue

Heartbreak I Life

As much as we love and care for our children, our lives are made up of choices that make us who we are. Through this process we become our true selves and grow in this magnificent journey called life.

Derek left us with a beautiful grandson who is his spitting image. Each day I have with Velzy it is as though Derek has returned to our family and me. I know that Velzy will carry the burden and legacy of his father's life, one filled with the seeds of greatness and hope. Much like his father, Velzy sees the world through his own unique point of view, taking notice of things most of our family will never see or understand.

I often ask, "Was Derek's death an act of selfishness, or was it his way of giving his ultimate love for his son to carry on?"

I know that all the takeaways I have experienced in my life border on devastation, financial failure, divorce, and business losses, but losing a son—a child—is life changing. Experiencing and somehow embracing each heartbreak has led me to what is ultimately available to each of us if we don't give up: a comeback.

A verse that has rung clear with me through the years is: "Don't worry about doing good, for at the proper time, ye shall receive a harvest if you do not give up" (Galatians 6:9). Life and death are intertwined with all the horrors, mysteries, magic, and wonders of life as they strengthen the human heart.

There is a reason that God limits our days—to make each day precious so that we can appreciate and live life to its fullest. My life was filled with dreams and words from *Man of La Mancha* that always inspired me in life's journey:

"The Impossible Dream"

To dream the impossible dream

To fight the unbeatable foe

To bear with unbearable sorrow

To run where the brave dare not go

To right the unrightable wrong

To love pure and chaste from afar

To try when your arms are too weary

To reach the unreachable star

This is my quest, to follow that star

No matter how hopeless, no matter how far

To fight for the right without question or pause

To be willing to march into hell for a heavenly cause

And I know if I'll only be true to this glorious quest

That my heart will lie peaceful and calm

When I am laid to my rest

And the world will be better for this

That one man scorned and covered with scars

Still strove with his last ounce of courage

To reach the unreachable stars.

Testimonials

Most people would say that the death of a child is one of the worst things that could ever happen to an individual. Yet, comfort for the surviving parent, if it happens at all, is too often given by people who know so little about how to help.

This is why Gene's book is of such great value. Gene painstakingly records and gives the reader a glimpse of how to survive the journey of unbelievable loss, grief and misery. To read this book is to become aware that the struggle with addiction is one of the most tragic realities that exist in our nation. If we ever hope to break the epidemic of drug addiction, in what has become one of our country's greatest tragedies, we must end the silence and start discussing honestly and openly the full scope of the problem and open up dialogue about how to help those escape and survive such addictions.

As a family member, I too have been rendered helpless and suffered the soul-destroying grief associated with loving an addict. Unlike Gene, I have not had to process the mind-numbing finality of losing a child. I greatly admire the courage and strength that it took for Nalbandian to share his story and journey with all parents. The warmth, authenticity and compassion that he exhibits in real life shines forth in every page.

Tyra Demateis

"I first met Gene Nalbandian as a consultant to a company he was the visionary founder of. His business acumen and enthusiasm is infectious. Our business relationship soon grew to a personal friendship, in part based on our common faith.

As businesspersons, community members, spouses, and parents, we each face unexpected life events, many outside of our control. Gene's book is a testimony to his search for what is good and the truth and leaves me hopeful for my future.

I have no doubt that when Gene meets his Maker face to face, He will say, "Well done my good and faithful servant."

John B. Withers, Partner
California Strategies, LLC

A fine story of achievement by an individual who never took no, and adapted to changing circumstances even after the suicide of his son.

Heartwarming life experiences for someone who always managed to come out on top. A good read about life and its success, and one major setback.

Assemblyman Walter J. Karabian (Ret.)
Former Majority Leader

Part of the proceeds of this book will be donated to continue Gene's effort toward assisting young children in Armenia born with severe deformities that are in need of specialized medical care.

Gene is developing a fund in memory of his son Derek to help teenagers afflicted with drug addiction.